Achieving Maximum Value from Information Systems

Wiley Series in Information Systems

Editors

Achieving Maximum Value
From Information Systems:
A Process Approach

DAN REMENYI
MICHAEL SHERWOOD-SMITH
with
TERRY WHITE

JOHN WILEY & SONS
Chichester · New York · Weinheim · Brisbane · Singapore · Toronto

National   01243 779777
International   (+44) 1243 779777
e-mail (for orders and customer service enquiries):
cs-books@wiley.co.uk
Visit our Home Page on http://www.wiley.co.uk
or http://www.wiley.com

Other Wiley Editorial Offices

John Wiley & Sons, Inc., 605 Third Avenue,
New York, NY 10158-0012, USA

Weinheim • Brisbane • Singapore • Toronto

Library of Congress Cataloguing-in-Publication Data
Available on request

British Library Cataloguing in Publication Data
A catalogue record for this book is available from the British Library

ISBN 0-471-97500-1

Produced from camera-ready copy supplied by TechTrans Limited.
Printed and bound in Great Britain by Biddles Limited, Guildford and Kings
Lynn.
This book is printed on acid-free paper responsibly manufactured from
sustainable forestation, for which at least two trees are planted for each one
used for paper production.

Contents

Foreword

The management of information systems (IS) benefits is an open research issue which has recently become a centre of concern for many IS professionals as they experience increasing pressure to demonstrate value from IT investments. Failure to do so has often lead to the end of a promising career or the outsourcing of IS services to a third party. This book addresses this very important aspect of IS management - a topic that has exercised the academic, practitioner and consulting communities for many years, and one which is still far from being resolved. The authors adopt a novel approach in that they attempt to integrate the IS value issue and the benefit management issue with the IS development process. In doing this they have called on some of the concepts and underlying philosophy of the post-modern management movement in order to explain the dynamic nature of IS outcome identification, stakeholder commitment and benefit realisation. The use of post-modern management thinking allows the authors to take more directly into account the importance of organisational issues in developing their approach to IS benefit realisation. Their approach culminates in the development of a reasonably detailed framework which may aid managers in the attainment of a benefit realisation programme. I welcome the contribution made by the authors in this challenging area. Theirs has been an ambitious task which they have tackled head-on. While they have made substantial progress, like the myth of Sisyphus, this job is an unending one. I, therefore, wish them well as they continue their work, and I also wish the many IS students, academics, practitioners and consultants well in applying the lessons that can be gleaned from this book. In so doing, they will in turn help to develop our understanding of this complex topic still further.

BOB GALLIERS
Chairman, Warwick Business School
University of Warwick

Series Preface

The information systems community has grown considerably since 1984, when we first started the Wiley Series in Information Systems. We are pleased to be part of the growth of the field, and believe that this series of books is playing an important role in the intellectual development of the discipline. The primary objective of the series is to publish scholarly works which reflect the best of research in the information systems community.

As the information systems field matures, there is an increased need to carry the results of its growing body of research into practice. The series desires to publish research results that speak to important needs in the development and management of information systems and our editorial mission recognises explicitly the need for research to inform the practice and management of information systems. Achieving Maximum Value from Information Systems: A Process Approach tackles the perplexing are of information systems evaluation through a unique blend of theory and practice. The infrequency of post implementation reviews or periodic bench-marking of established information systems is one of those glaring examples of technology managers' failure to 'practise what they preach'. We should expect investments in information technologies to be just as carefully scrutinised as other aspects of a firm's operations – no matter how difficult the measurement of benefits may be.

The authors take a post-modern approach to the problem of evaluating information systems investments, emphasising the need for multiple perspectives and multiple evaluations in a continuous participative evaluation process of active benefit realisation. The result is a well developed programme that combines theoretical grounding with practical experience to address an enduring and increasingly significant problem for information systems managers. We believe it will be a great benefit to information technology executives as well as to advanced graduate students.

RUDY HIRSHHEIM   DICK BOLAND
University of Houston,   *Case Western Reserve University*
Texas   *Ohio*

PREVIOUS VOLUMES IN THE SERIES

Preface

It is probably true to say that there has always been a question mark over the issue of the value of business computing. However, in the past both business managers and information systems professionals have been able to justify information systems investment without having to prove a business case and furthermore without much attempt to demonstrate, afterwards, the actual value generated by the information system. Increasingly this is no longer acceptable to business managers, or for that matter to information systems professionals themselves, who need to be assured that corporate funds are being spent wisely. As a result considerable energy and resources have been spent on researching suitable ways of evaluating information systems during the past 10 years.

But the issue is not only the creation of a business case and the measurement of what takes place after the investment. It has become clear that the difference between success and failure with information systems, and thus the level of return which they produce, lies to a large extent in the way the systems are developed and implemented. This is simple because if they are not developed with a strong focus on benefit delivery then the prospect of systems being used to create a benefit stream is limited.

The seeds of this book were unknowingly sown at a chance meeting of the authors at the 1991 Annual Joint Conference of the Irish Computer Society and British Computer Society. Dan Remenyi had been working on strategic information systems and had just co-authored his book on Measuring and Managing IT Benefits. Michael Sherwood-Smith had just completed his doctorate on information systems evaluation and had begun working on the evaluation of information systems, in the context of building information systems which are of value to their eventual users. The collaboration flourished and was extended to Terry White who joined up much later in 1996. This book is the result. The book is a distillation of the authors' world-wide experience in information systems management in business and consultancy, as well as published academic research in the field, ABR research seminars and focus groups.

This book proposes an approach to the development and implementation of information systems which is referred to as Active Benefit Realisation and which can make a major impact on the performance of funds invested in information systems. Being able to ensure that the funds spent on information systems investment make an adequate return for the organisation will substantially improve the position and the prestige of the information systems professional.

But the application of Active Benefit Realisation is not a trivial matter and will require a high degree of commitment and a considerable amount of effort to provide the approach with a reasonable chance of success.

Acknowledgements

The authors would like to acknowledge the hundreds of practising managers who have contributed some of their years of experience by discussing the issues in this book with the authors. We would also like to thank the academic reviewers who have given us the benefit of their valuable input and comments.

Collaboration and research on this book was supported by Forbairt-Irish Science and Innovation Support Directorate (Grant SC/96/617)

About the Authors

Dan Remenyi PhD has spent more than 20 years working in the field of corporate computing and information systems working with computers and communications as an IS professional, business consultant and end-user. In recent years he has specialised in the areas of strategic information systems, measuring the effectiveness of information systems and technology forecasting. He has authored and co-authored more than 20 textbooks in the field of information systems.

Michael Sherwood-Smith PhD, FICS is currently the Head of the Department of Computer Science at University College Dublin (UCD). He worked for 20 years in data processing and management with international companies (Nestlé, W.R. Grace & Unilever). Since 1981 he has been in the Computer Science Department at UCD involved in teaching and research. He has been a Project Director on European Commission research projects for ten years. His doctoral research was in the field of evaluation of information systems. He has published several papers as well as lectured and consulted in this field. He is a past Chairman of the Irish Computer Society (ICS).

Terry White BSc(Hons), MCom was originally a geologist who moved into information systems in the area of Facilities Management. Since then he has concentrated on the management issues in information systems environments as well as on the management of IS people and the business interface. He recently left Afrox Limited where he worked as an information systems manager for the past 13 years. In 1995 he completed a Master of Commerce Degree in Information Systems and has already begun his research towards a doctorate.

1

An Introduction to Active Benefit Realisation

'We need the courage to let go of the old world, to relinquish most of what we have cherished, to abandon our interpretations about what does and doesn't work'

Margaret Wheatley, Leadership and the New Science, 1992.

1. INTRODUCTION

This book proposes a post-modern way of thinking about the management of information systems (IS) and especially information systems development which is referred to as Active Benefit Realisation (ABR). The book describes a contingency approach and a framework for a co-creation and/or co-evolutionary[1] approach to information systems development and management incorporating all the main stakeholders. Coming into the 21st century the effective use of Information

---

[1] A co-evolutionary approach means that all the stakeholders' interests are considered in deciding how to proceed with an information systems development. This needs to be contrasted with either the information systems people deciding what the eventual user needs and producing an information system for them, or the user demanding an information system without understanding what is possible or desirable from the different points of view of the other stakeholders.

Technology (IT) is seen by many as a key differentiator between the successful enterprise and the mediocre. However, for many organisations IT-enabled business success is a holy grail which has yet to be discovered. It is now realised that the application of IT is very difficult and the objective is not to throw technology at the problem to devise an elegant technological solution but to use technology to actively realise business benefits. This involves blending the use of the technology with the current business objectives of the enterprise, the management of the development of the information system to give business value to the organisation and fitting the use of the information technology to the corporate culture, style and aspirations of the organisation, its management and its staff.

ABR is an approach to information systems development which focuses on achieving the maximum value from information systems investment by focusing on the delivery of business benefits, which it achieves through the involvement of all the appropriate stakeholders. These benefits are realised through the process of continuous participative evaluation[2].

The subject of ABR is important because it is increasingly clear that the current approach to information systems development and management has not always produced satisfactory results. Specifically computer systems take too long to develop, cost too much to produce (Allingham and O'Connor 1992; Lester and Willcocks 1993; Banker and Kemerer 1991) and are frequently not perceived to deliver the business benefits which were intended (Heygate 1993; Attewell 1993; Brynjolfsson 1993; Wilson 1993; Hitt and Brynjolfsson 1994; Remenyi *et al.* 1995).

---

[2] It is realised that the book suggests a generic approach which will have to be modified depending on whether support systems, factory systems, strategic systems or turnaround systems (McFarlan 1984) are being developed. The actual way ABR is applied will also be affected by the state of information systems maturity and other organisational variables.

The speed of delivery of information systems solutions is now regularly seen as a limiting factor in business agility and flexibility. Many of these circumstances and complaints are not new, having been a central challenge for information systems management for the past 30 years but they continue to be a major problem in many organisations today.

There have been continuous attempts to improve both the efficiency and effectiveness with which computer systems are conceptualised, developed and commissioned and although considerable progress has been made the situation is still plagued by many problems. As we leave the second half of the 1990s, these problems require an urgent resolution as it becomes more and more apparent that traditional information system methods no longer fit the way organisations need to conduct their business in an ever increasingly competitive environment.

One of the clearest and most biting statements of discontent with information systems performance was made by Computer Weekly (1991) which stated:

> 'Time has run out for IT managers who act like a protected species. Their three-fold failure to under-stand the business they are supposed to be part of, to communicate with their business colleagues, and to deliver cost effective systems has led to a collapse of faith in the IT department itself, and a determination by business managers to find alternative solutions to their computing needs.'

Previous attempts to resolve these problems have generally not been successful because the real causes of the problems have not been fully understood. As a result of recent research, there is now a growing understanding of the drivers[3] of successful information system development and performance, and methods are evolving to improve the delivery of appropriate information systems that return real business benefits to the organisation.

The evidence to support the arguments presented in this book is drawn both from the general literature on information systems management and from conceptual and empirical work done in the information systems field. The theoretical foundation originates from the work conducted by academics such as Keen (1975), Hirschheim and Smithson (1988), Currie (1989), Symons (1991), Walsham (1993), Lester and Willcocks(1993), Farbey *et al.* (1995), Scriven (1991:a&b), House (1993), Finne *et al.* (1995), Rebien (1996) and Ward *et al.* (1996) which has led to the formulation of a continuous evaluation process to the management of information systems development. The approach is based on several different strands of thought, central to which are the concepts of *post-modernism*[4] and *formative evaluation.*

---

[3] There is a number of drivers of successful information systems development and performance which are discussed in some detail later in this book. The key driver is perhaps best summarised in the term, continuous participative evaluation, which involves people collaborating for success, the focusing on business benefits, and regular evaluation. All these will be explained in detail later in the book, and the corporate environment and culture which makes this possible.

[4] The authors have taken some licence in their use the term *post-modernism.* According to the Fontana Dictionary of Modern Thought, 'post-modernism is an increasingly familiar if still controversial term for defining or suggesting the overall character or direction of experimental tendencies in Western arts, architecture, etc. since the 1940s or 1950s and particularly more recent developments associated with post-industrial society.' In this book the authors use the term post-modernism to suggest new and experimental directions in management thinking, and of course especially management thinking as it applies to information systems development.

1.1 Post-modern information systems development

The post-modernist concept as it is applied to information systems development concentrates on a number of issues, one of the most important being what is described later in this book as the contingent mind-set to systems development. In simple terms this means that information systems goal-posts[5] may change and developers need to be prepared for this. A programme of continuous participative evaluation is introduced to manage the changes and to ensure that goal-post changes are recognised as early as possible and that disruption resulting from changes is minimised. This results in a strong preference for phased delivery of information systems.

Furthermore the ABR approach recognises a shifting of the focus of information systems management away from being the sole responsibility of the information systems department to being the shared responsibility of a group of the main information system stakeholders. This approach recognises that information systems do not, per se, deliver any benefits but they rather facilitate improvements to business performance (Ward *et al.* 1996) which in turn may result in the production of business benefits. This being the case, so-called information systems benefit delivery is the responsibility of the management who requested and commissioned the information system.

---

[5] Generally goal-post changes are usually regarded as aberrations, which where possible need to be avoided, and significant management trauma is experienced as the new goals are missed, and targets are not achieved. There is now a growing recognition that the assumptions behind the static nature of goals are not only unrealistic, but are detrimental to organisational progress and to the achievement of significant benefits which most initiatives or investments should produce. These old unrealistic assumptions of stasis which have largely incorrectly defined management reality and thus influenced behaviours, need to change if we are to remain in touch with the rapid pace of business, social and political change faced by organisations as they enter the 21st century.

1.2 Formative evaluation

The concept of formative evaluation is central to ABR because it is through the dialogue between the main stakeholders which this approach to evaluation creates that information systems projects are kept either on track or within acceptable boundaries. As proposed in this book formative evaluation is a process whereby all the relevant stakeholders may contribute their views and values as to how the proposed system should be developed. This process requires regular review meetings during which an open attitude allows a comprehensive and meaningful discussion of all the key issues related to the proposed information system.

To be successful with formative evaluation it is necessary to establish a mind-set which welcomes suggestions of possible change. It is also most important that there is no attempt to limit the source of such suggestions to executives only. The views of all competent stakeholders should be carefully listened to. Sometimes formative evaluation is referred to as learning evaluation as its intent is to improve performance and thus achieve a more satisfactory outcome.

1.3 Business benefits

Inherent to a post-modern approach to information systems development is the notion that information systems benefits should not be defined in terms of simple financial returns alone, but rather be seen as a composite of issues which deliver real business value to a number of different stakeholders in the organisation, some of which may be intangible, i.e. cannot be reduced to financial numbers. Thus some of the benefits will be expressed in financial terms while others will be defined in terms of organisational issues which sometimes may not easily lend themselves to financial quantification. Of course there is a need to clearly state how these objectives relate to corporate financial objectives and targets as well as how individuals will actually use the systems to improve their performance and thus obtain benefits for the organisation.

1.4 Co-evolution and participation

The ABR approach to information systems management recognises that the all too familiar tension between information systems departments and other corporate functions is counter-productive and promotes the involvement of a group of stakeholders, all of whom play a co-evolutionary role in the development of information systems to produce real business solutions (Remenyi and Sherwood-Smith 1996:a&b). The main purpose behind the co-evolutionary approach is to

'destroy the us-versus-them barriers and distinctions' (Wiseman 1996)

which plagues so much of our organisational world. In effect an ABR approach requires a mind-set enthusiastic to active participation, and a much more disciplined framework to information systems development.

2. ABR AND ITS SCOPE

ABR, as proposed in this book focuses on achieving the maximum value from information systems investment by ensuring that the information systems development process, from conceptualisation to benefit delivery, is managed efficiently and effectively in order to achieve the required outcomes. As presently envisaged ABR is an information systems development approach or framework. The authors specifically do not wish to make a claim that ABR is a methodology as this would require the creation or development of detailed procedures. ABR explicitly puts in evidence the building blocks and ethos for realising benefits from information systems.

At the core of ABR is the notion of the information systems outcome, which may be defined as the business result, including the benefit stream, of the information system after it has been successfully commissioned and implemented. Using ABR, the information system is defined in broad business terms, largely in terms of benefits, which in some cases may be fairly general in nature. The term *outcome space* is used to describe these business benefits.

ABR may be understood as the process by which an information systems development project proceeds from the initiation point to an acceptable location in the outcome space in order to achieve suitable benefits for the organisation. As the development proceeds formative evaluation is used to ensure that the project remains within the boundaries which will eventually lead the information system to deliver the required benefit stream, as shown in Figure 1.1.

The post-modern ideas underpinning ABR and concepts such as contingency, continuous participative evaluation, co-evolution are perfectly valid for activities within the information systems environment. Furthermore, numerous informants with whom ABR has been discussed have commented on the universality of this approach to organisational problems in general.

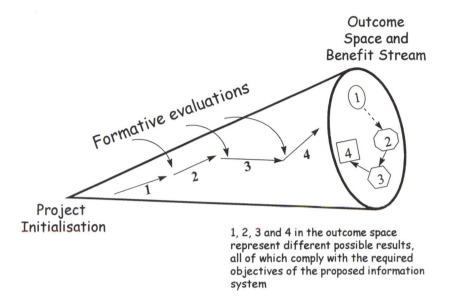

Outcome
Space and
Benefit Stream

Formative evaluations

Project
Initialisation

1, 2, 3 and 4 in the outcome space
represent different possible results,
all of which comply with the required
objectives of the proposed information
system

Figure 1.1: Outcome space and formative evaluation

3. SUMMARY AND CONCLUSIONS

ABR offers an opportunity to improve the performance of information systems development management and thus to move towards achieving the maximum value from information systems investment. However the implementation of ABR is not a simple matter and thus offers a challenge.

An ABR programme takes time and especially management time to set up and to establish as a routine way of implementing information systems. This approach to information systems development may increase the management cost but this may be contained and result in a far higher level of benefits being achieved[6]. Although the concepts underpinning ABR are neither

---

[6] There are actually no data available on the costs of implementing ABR. However, a number of informants have pointed out that information systems project overheads

new nor old[7] the application of ABR is only now beginning to be applied in organisations in the last years of the twentieth century. There are many reasons why the ideas behind ABR have not yet been extensively put into practice. The most important of these reasons is that, at the heart of ABR is the admission that change is a natural part of the organisation's life. In turn this means that all forecasts, estimates and plans have to be by their very nature contingent. Consequently this impacts sales people's commitment to their quotas, machine operators' targets for their hourly or daily output, the number of deliveries made by the truck drivers, etc. This is seen by some top managers as opening the door to a lack of control and consequently disorder and organisations have a very low tolerance for any idea which could lead to this possibility (Wheatley 1992).

There are indications that ABR is currently being recognised as a far more effective approach to information systems development than any previous framework and it is expected that the growth in its use over the next few years will be substantial. The potential benefits of ABR are truly substantial and the downside risk of implementing this approach is very small.

---

may cost from a few percent to maybe as much as 20% of the cost of the whole project.

[7] The idea of formative evaluation has its roots in the 19th century in both the United Kingdom and the United States of America (Chelimsky 1985), but it is relatively new to business especially information systems management. Originally formative evaluation was a technique developed to help improve the performance of government and social initiatives especially in the field of education and health (Scriven 1967; Patton 1986).

2

IS Management: The Need for a Post-Modern Approach

'The difficulty lies, not in the new ideas, but in escaping from the old ones'

John Maynard Keynes, The General Theory of Employment, Interest and Money, 1936.

1. INTRODUCTION

There is a growing belief that there is a major misfit or dis-connect between information systems development by traditional methods and the expectations and requirements of business and that this situation is an increasing problem to executives as they attempt to achieve and sustain a competitive advantage (Lincoln 1990; Earl 1992). It is the elimination of this misfit or dis-connect which this chapter and this book addresses. ABR proposes an approach which will substantially improve this situation.

1.1 Speed of systems development

Both the time taken to develop information systems solutions, and the flexibility of the development process present problems to the business. In addition there is also the issue of cost. One of the reasons for this may be attributed to the increased need to respond quickly to the market. Stalk and Hout (1990) and Sherman (1994) believe that contrary to the theory established by Porter (1985) and Treacy and Wiersema (1993) quality and price have ceased to be differentiators in business competitiveness, and rather that speed of implementation of new ideas now defines the edge.

This view is also clearly supported by Pritchett (1994) when he states:

> 'We live in an impatient world, with fierce competition
> and fleeting opportunities. Organisations that are lean,
> agile, and quick to respond, clearly have the edge.'

In many organisations this sense of urgency has not permeated down to the information systems department. In fact a central problem is that traditional information systems development methods tend to be a barrier to speed to market, agility, short cycle times and innovation. This has in part been due to the lack of tools available, but also an acceptance of the attitude of *more haste, less speed.* Increasingly this view is no longer acceptable.

1.2 Appropriateness of functionality

The traditional information systems development process requires accurate specification of user requirements, sign-off on specification documents, and some time later, perhaps six months, one year, two years or worse, user acceptance testing. Research suggests that users frequently do not know exactly what they want, change their minds, and are more concerned with results and outputs than with the production of a system. As a result the traditional systems development method has been far from successful:

> 'Of all software projects incorporating over 64,000 lines of code, 25% failed to deliver anything; 60% were over budget and behind schedule, and only 1% met requirements on time and on budget.' (Beam, 1994)

The traditional cry from the information systems profession that 'We cannot deliver the requirements because they keep changing!' may comfort information system people, but it evokes little or no sympathy from other parts of the business.

The post-modernist view of information systems development based on the contingency notion, recognises that organisations cannot stop the world from changing during the period of information systems development. The best such organisations can do is adapt quickly. The lack of information system outcomes which are appropriate to the environment when a system is eventually delivered, as opposed to the time it was originally specified, clearly highlights the unacceptability of information system development methods.

The whole economic, social and political environment as well as the business organisations therein are moving rapidly away from 'steady-state' ways of thinking. The environment of the late 1990s requires a positive attitude towards continuous change. This notion of fast and continuous change has been expressed by many writers including Peters (1987), Handy (1989), Foster (1986) and Wiersema (1996).

So the nature of the deliverables of information systems needs to be capable of changing and adjusting with the changing nature of business needs. This implies that the full range of possible deliverables will probably never be completed in the way they were originally envisaged. Organisations have to be prepared to accept moving goal-posts and the resultant change as the normal way of preparing systems.

1.3 Cost and value of information system deliverables

To intensify the crisis in the information systems community, information systems departments have required increasingly large sums of cash to sustain their activities. The amounts of funds involved have increased year by year as higher and higher performance technology has been offered by the vendors. It is now clear that in many organisations more than half of all the funds invested in business are consumed by the information systems function (Willcocks 1994).

2. INFORMATION SYSTEMS IN THE CONTEXT OF BUSINESS THEORY

Although there is considerable dissatisfaction with the management of the information systems function in many organisations, it is important to see this in the context of a growing concern with the way some of the largest businesses and public institutions in the western world are managed today. Many leading firms which were believed to be models of excellent management are no longer performing well. And it is not entirely clear whether this is due to a lack of competence on the part of the management teams of these organisations, or more seriously, the fact that the well established business paradigms which have functioned very well in the past, are no longer appropriate to the last decade of the twentieth century.

There is sufficient evidence to suggest that there have been a number of serious mistakes in how some firms have ignored fundamental changes in the marketplace over the last few years and furthermore the size of the errors made suggest that more is wrong than poor judgement or lack of care.

These unsatisfactory corporate performances have led a number of business theorists, such as Pascale (1990), to comment on the apparent lack of understanding of what is required to sustain success:

'Owing to the inadequacy of our understanding as to what sustains success, we are unable to help organisations sustain performance with any reliability. This is evident when we take stock of how poorly our assessment and predictions stack up with results.'

An even stronger argument is offered by Wiersema (1996)

'In the 1970s and the early 1980s many companies had to admit that they didn't know how to make durable goods or deliver reliable services. Defect rates as high as 20 or 30 percent were common, and apathetic service was the norm.'

Thus the need for a paradigm which directly addresses the issues of how to instigate, implement and manage change is perceived as critical to corporate success in the mid-1990s. In the words of Business Week (1992):

'What becomes essential is a fresh new mind-set, a new way of perceiving the role of information technology in business.'

This new paradigm, which encourages information systems to play a central role in business, and which anticipates and accommodates a high level of inevitable change is what the authors refer to as the post-modern approach to business and management.

3. PRE-MODERNISM, MODERNISM AND POST-MODERNISM

To understand the post-modernistic approach to business and management it is necessary to review the original meaning of pre-modernism, modernism and post-modernism.

3.1 Pre-modernism

The basic tenet of what is referred to now as pre-modernism was that human understanding was a function of revealed truths. Truths were revealed or handed down by those in authority which were either religious sources or in some cases by superstition. Thus pre-modern understanding was without much scientific basis and was frequently compromised by human feelings. Pre-modernists believe that the purpose of life is largely revealed through nature. In a pre-modern environment explanations of the world are subjective or personal and there is little accuracy or ability to predict or control.

3.2 Modernism

According to modernists, science provides a knowledge of reality which is exact and efficient. Modern men and women are capable of being rationally detached individuals. Reality consists of knowable quantities of the facts of matter. Nothing in the world escapes the grasp of reason. There is only one way of knowing and that is through the neutral processes of observation, measurement and argument which is referred to as science or the scientific method. Science is accurate and provides explanations as well as the ability to predict and control (Wheatley 1992). The world is nothing more than a series of physical causes and effects. There is no limit to human rational conquests. According to this view of life modern humans can be completely free from irrational superstitions. To the modernist, science is a value free activity which inevitably leads to the truth being discovered. Such an approach to the world proclaims that numbers are the ultimate test of objectivity (Gould 1992). Of course this view is an entirely positivist understanding of science which has been referred to by Medawar (1986) as a period piece'. By the end of the 20th century this scientific view of the world, especially as it applies to people and to organisations is being severely questioned.

In fact the positivist approach is being increasingly questioned as Gould (1992) points out:

> 'Facts are not pure and unsullied bits of information; culture also influences what we see and how we see it.'

And according to Jung (1995):

> 'Science works with concepts of averages which are far too general to do justice to the subjective variety of an individual life.'

Another interesting opinion on the limits of the positivistic approach is described by Medawar (1986) as follows:

> 'Boswell-like, I once asked Karl Popper to express in a sentence the quintessence of the teaching of positivism. He at once replied: "The world is all surface".'

Clearly the modernist view of the world has, to the extent that it is based on determinism and reductionism, some important limitations.

3.3 Post-modernism

According to post-modernists there is no single reality and thus there is no reliable universal and permanent knowledge. The current understanding of the universe is not superior to previous versions but rather, only different. All human ideas, including this one, are dependent upon prior judgements about what exists. Humans actually create what they want to see as concepts, and values are filters which determine what is observed. Thus human reality is not only experienced in terms of forces and materials but also in terms of contexts and values. Human behaviour in particular is about much more than rationality. This applies to both individuals and organisations. Human behaviour is about feelings and about purposes and needs and values. The post-modernist believes that there is no way of looking at the world which is value free.

Thus, to the post-modernist, individuals can choose to see or know the world in different ways. Science is just one human way of looking at the world or reality. There are other ways however. This way of thinking suggests that science only interprets and it is not intrinsically neutral. Scientific theories are open to endless revision and current scientific ideas are nothing more than human work in progress. Recognising that humans cannot have a pure or unbiased picture of the world is one of the most important tenets which underlies the concepts of post-modernism. What is obvious to one individual is not necessarily obvious to another. Furthermore knowledge is a function of language, context and imagination and, as mentioned above has always to be regarded as tentative or provisional. There is no escaping the fact that knowledge has to be interpreted. Human meaning may be compared to architecture. It is always a function of when it was created or designed and where it was created or designed.

Post-modernism prefers not to package ideas, but rather leaves them for individual interpretation and acceptance. This paradigm implies that most human and organisational activities are not deterministic and that the reductionist approach borrowed from the modernists is of little value in developing understanding. The post-modernist attempts to establish a more integrated and holistic view of reality.

Of course it is sometimes argued that too much is made of the distinction between modernism and post-modernism and that this approach is a passing fad and thus it is not to be taken seriously. However Habermas (1994) takes a different view:

> 'the "posties" are not only deft opportunists with their noses to the wind; as seismographers tracking the spirit of the age, they must also be taken seriously'.

Post-modernism represents an important shift in 20th century thinking.

3.4 Pre-modern business and management principles

The notion of pre-modern business and management principles refers to the economic thinking which prevailed in the 17th and 18th centuries. This period was dominated by the Mercantilists in England and the Physiocrats in France. Writers such as Thomas Mann and Sir Frances Stuart argued that wealth was directly related to the ownership of precious metals and a favourable balance of trade. Thus they proclaimed that manufacturing should be prohibited in the colonies. The Physiocrats, led by the writings of François Quesney, believed that real wealth could only be obtained from agricultural surpluses. To their way of thinking manufacturing did not create wealth but rather distributed it. Clearly there was no scientific or objective basis to any of these pre-modern doctrines.

3.5 Modern business and management principles

Modern business and management principles began to play an
important role towards the end of the 19th century with the
writings of W. F. Taylor, which he referred to as scientific
management, and with the implementation of much of his
thinking by Henry Ford. Taylorism and Fordism are believed by
many to be the driving forces behind Western society's
economic growth in the 20th century. Based on the thinking of
Adam Smith and other classical economists the work of Taylor
and Ford operationalised micro-economics into management
theory and practice. These ideas, which largely rely on
knowledge derived from the scientific process, have underpinned much of Western management thinking and success until
the last quarter of this century. It is most important to state that
modern business and management principles have been highly
successful and are clearly responsible for the massive
improvement in the standard of living of individuals throughout
many parts of the world.

3.6 Post-modern business and management principles

Post-modern business and management principles began to
emerge in the 1970s. This thinking suggested that the current
orthodoxy in management approaches which was built on
objective scientific management with little or no consideration
for the inherent ambiguity in many business matters and
situations and especially the lack of understanding and empathy
for the people and organisational issues involved, was not
working as well as it was expected to. This was particularly
evidenced when Western firms found themselves in direct
competition with Japanese organisations. This situation was well
described by Konosuke Matsushita (1982) when he said:

'We are going to win and the industrial west is going to lose out; there's not much you can do about it because the reasons for your failure are within yourselves. Your firms are built on the Taylor model, even worse, so are your heads. With your bosses doing the thinking while the workers wield screwdrivers, you're convinced deep down that this is the right way to run a business. For the essence of management is getting the ideas out of the heads of the bosses and into the hands of labour.'

Of course the Japanese approach to management was not entirely unscientific nor was it particularly post-modern. But Western organisations' contact with Japanese competitors started a re-thinking of old assumptions about management philosophies and methods. However, it is quite reasonable to suggest that post-modern management thinking is in some senses a reaction to problems encountered by the rigorous application of Taylorism and Fordism and others, which recognises that management requires much more than simple objective scientific analysis.

Specifically in the business and management context post-modernism suggest the following:

1. The notion that there is no uniquely correct answer to most or perhaps even to any particular business or management problem. There are simply different viewpoints which change and develop over time. Thus to a post-modern manager an experimental and incremental approach to solving a problem would make most sense. In practical terms this implies that managers have to live with a high degree of ambiguity and that it is therefore essential to take business and management risks. From this it follows that it is necessary to reward individuals for the outcomes for which they are responsible.

2. The particular meaning of ideas, including both rational and non-rational, is a central consideration as is the relationship of the ideas to one another. As meaning is most important in this new management paradigm it needs to be continuously checked by the participants of any discourse. A direct implication of this thinking is that corporate governance by shared values is far superior to governance by power or status imposed control.

3. There is the notion that business and management and the supporting systems thereof are intrinsically complex and thus there is always a degree of ambiguity. This is especially true when the human dimension is taken into account. This means that holistic solutions to problems should be sought where possible. The non-determinist nature of human behaviour and the systems affected by humans is admitted and attempts are made to accommodate this.

4. In this new thinking individual autonomy is highly regarded and therefore shared values are essential to keep a group together. The natural tension arising from difference and diversity in individuals is seen as a positive phenomenon. The diversity is channelled towards a process of co-creation and co-evolution in order to lead to a new level of creativity.

5. Heroic leaders are avoided. Post-heroic leadership which identifies the importance of networking and brokership is encouraged. The leadership role is defined in terms of the need to capture attention, create meaning, build trust and manage the self.

6. Underlying this new paradigm there is a sense of the need for change, growth, risk and urgency in which short term outcomes are balanced against, or within a context of long term values. Thus there is no position of stable equilibrium

but rather the notion of continuous or sometimes step wise improvements.

7. Context is all important, especially with regard to the establishment of values, as well as management principles and practices. All decisions need to be seen within the context in which the key players operate.

Although many of the ideas which constitute the post-modern approach to business and management have been discussed by both practitioners and consultants for quite some time, they are not yet in general practice[1]. Perhaps it will be in the field of information systems management, which is currently under such heavy scrutiny and pressure, where this new paradigm will first make a significant contribution.

4. FACTORS AFFECTING THE NEED FOR A POST-MODERN APPROACH TO INFORMATION SYSTEMS MANAGEMENT

To be able to appreciate how the post-modern approach to information systems works it is necessary to understand some of the inhibitors to successful information systems management.

---

[1] In fact during discussions with focus groups many informants express the view that they would be delighted to work in an organisation which would implement such management practices. It should also be said that although some informants said that they perceived some movement in their organisations towards post-modern thinking there was in general still a very long way to go before this approach became extensively accepted and practised.

4.1 The IS culture gap

It seems that there has always been a degree of tension between information systems departments and other functions in many, if not most organisations. This tension has been deep rooted and persistent over a considerable period of time and has probably been due to the fact that line managers have not really understood what has been required to produce high quality information systems, and information systems managers have failed to convince their colleagues as to the importance of the contribution made by information systems to the organisation. In addition information systems people have relied heavily on their own computer concepts, terms and language as the basis on which they were able or prepared to discuss the organisation's information requirements with senior line management. This has led, over the years, to major gaps of understanding and tension between the two groups[2]. This gap has been a major problem and is one of the direct causes of the need for formative evaluation or an active benefit realisation programme. Clearly neither side in this argument have taken a holistic view of the contribution which information systems can play in an organisation in the later years of the 20th century.

It is interesting to note that this tension between information systems people and the rest of the organisation persisted for at least three decades without there being a crisis, or even without this issue becoming a major focal point of debate. It is sometimes said that this reflected the fact that line management was just too intimidated to take on the computer boffins and to establish exactly what they were doing and why. However,

---

[2] It is true that all professions have their own language or jargon. However, it is increasingly accepted that jargon should not be used in discussing issues with others who are not fully conversant with the technical terms as at best it is a distraction and can frequently prevent the development of understandings.

computer people have had their critics and one of the early denunciations of computers and computer people was made by Townsend (1984) who summarised his views as follows:

'First get it through your head that computers are big, expensive, fast, dumb, adding-machine-typewriters. Then realise that most of the computer technicians that you are likely to meet or hire are complicators, not simplifiers. They're trying to make it look tough.'

Another strongly anti-computer people attitude was expressed very amusingly by Butler (1990) when he said:

'At present, the systems function is often thought of by its host organisation as rather like a small group of aliens living on a hostile Earth. The aliens can, through the powers the Earth-men barely understand, make themselves look and talk like Earth-men but they have no emotions, no hopes, no fears and they breed in unconventional ways! Eventually they might take over the world. Until then, they should be ignored as much as possible.'

Although fortunately some organisations are actively working on this problem and thus beginning to build bridges of trust and working partnerships between information systems staff, line managers and computer users, this distrust problem remains. In fact Grindley (1991) points out that the results of his research show that:

'The "Culture Gap" between those knowledgeable about IT and company managers and users in general is stated by 62% of IT directors to be their top problem.'

It has been very difficult for information systems management to respond to allegations such as these, because until recently there has been very little available in the way of theories and techniques to enable them to objectively evaluate their contribution to the running of the organisation. As a result of new management concepts this situation is beginning to change and information systems benefit realisation programmes are an important element in this change.

4.2 The traditional delivery approach

Another of the primary causes of the intense dissatisfaction with information systems is the traditional delivery approach to information systems which does not take the changing environment into account. The traditional information systems development life cycle (SDLC) when implemented in a highly structured way worked relatively well in more static environments during the 1970s and 1980s. However this method of producing systems has several inherent flaws one of which was the fact that during the justification stage, both users and information system practitioners sometimes found it difficult to identify real and measurable benefits (Silk 1990) and another was the notion of freezing the requirement.

The approach of post-modern management, as expressed by the process of ABR, recognises that the need to allow changes to the specification can eliminate many of the problems. This is because business and organisational change is central to the notion of post-modernism and this needs to be accommodated during the software development life cycle.

4.3 The emphasis on output rather than outcome

The emphasis on output[3] rather than outcome is another issue which caused major problems and which is inherent in traditional information systems management thinking. Post-modernism helps to refocus management attention on the issue of outcomes. When the business and information systems department develop a budget system, they may lose sight of the eventual business outcome. For example, the outcome of having a budgeting system is the achievement of controlled and aligned goals for future operations rather than simply the recording of planned and actual expenses. Outcome definition is frequently as difficult for information systems people as it is for management and eventual end users who can most easily appreciate the business outcomes. Bruns and McFarlan (1987) suggest how business outcomes differ from systems outputs in the list provided in Figure 2.1.

System Outputs	Business Outcome
Budgets	Goal definition
Production monitoring	Assurance of quality
Inventory & Sales	Speed and cost cutting
Payroll systems	Incentives and motivation

Figure 2.1: Business outcomes versus system outputs

---

[3] An information system output may be seen as a suite of programs, manuals and user tutorials and all the other supporting documentation. Outputs are normally physical manifestations of the system.

These authors assert that technology is organisationally neutral, a fact that is often missed by both information systems and the business. This view is very similar to Ward *et al.* (1996) when they said that information systems do not deliver benefits, but can only facilitate improved business performance if used in the proper manner. Thus it is not the technology which provides benefits, but the eventual end users when the information systems are put to work by them. However, regarding the technology as organisationally neutral is a dangerous stance to take. In fact, post-modernism would recognise that complete neutrality is impossible and that there will always be a complex interaction between technology processes and people. This is a corporate reality which must be managed in a disciplined and holistic way. Thus the inter-dependence of the information systems activity and the eventual user requires recognition and careful management from the outset to the system's outcome.

In a survey performed in 1992, Lederer and Sethi show that while there is general satisfaction with information system outputs, there is overall dissatisfaction with the achievement of the desired outcome through the 'carrying out of the plan' which is shown in Figure 2.2. This reflects the fact that information systems are not delivering adequate business benefits.

	Satisfied	**Neutral**	**Dissatisfied**
Methodology	54%	23%	23%
Process	48%	17%	35%
Output	55%	17%	28%
Carrying out the plan	32%	15%	53%

Figure 2.2: Information system output versus desired outcome

There is clearly a number of reasons why there is this gap between systems delivery and subsequent benefit delivery and one possible explanation of this discontinuity, expressed as a difference between information system output and the achievement of a business outcome is provided by Hansen and Wernerfelt (1989) who state:

> 'Both economic and organisational factors are significant independent determinants of firm performance. Organisational factors explain about twice as much variance in profit rates as economic factors.'

Organisational factors relate to human resources, and to goal accomplishment. Information systems whose success have been defined in economic terms only, are unlikely to achieve the business outcome.

Post-modernist information systems executives take a much more benefit or outcome orientated view of information systems and thus helps alleviate some of the problems.

4.4 Cost and return on investment

There is ample evidence that senior line management is dissatisfied with the performance of the information system function with respect to their cost effectiveness and return on investment. Lincoln (1990) pointed out that:

> 'The past few years have seen a marked shift in the attitude of senior executives towards the use of information technology. No longer are expenditures seen as low and investments "acts of faith". Now executives require that their information systems are both profitable and can be shown to be profitable.'

This attitude was triggered by a number of factors, not the least of which was the scale of the investment in IT and the apparently low return it was earning. According to Keen (1991):

> 'throughout the 1980s compounded expenditure on IT grew in the region of 350% yet productivity in manufacturing and services over the same period showed an increase of between 3% and 15%.'

Supporting these researchers, and perhaps dealing the greatest insult of all to information systems and information technologists came a comment from the Economist which proclaimed that manufacturers who purchased information technology in the late 1970s and the early 1980s earned such a low return on their money invested that they:

> 'would have done better ... to have invested that same capital in almost any other part of their businesses.'
> (Economist, 1991)

This accusation is reinforced by the fact that through the 1980s while computer expenditure was expanding at a rapid rate, productivity, especially in the United States of America, was hardly growing at all (Krugman 1992). Figure 2.3 is a chart of United States' productivity growth showing the abysmal performance in the 1980s. In fact, as may be seen from the chart, the two decades since 1970 have been the worst for United States' productivity performance for the preceding 100 years, despite enormous investment in information systems.

However many observers of the information technology industry would argue that the Economist Newspaper was not being fair as there are several possible reasons why the return on this sort of investment does not appear to be high, one of which relates to the misuse or mismanagement of the technology.

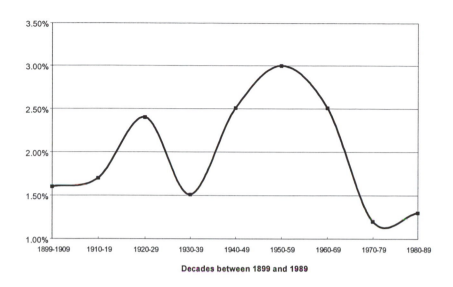

Figure 2.3: USA productivity statistics for 1889-1989

There are two basic arguments concerning the mismanagement of information technology. Firstly it is frequently said that many of the applications which have been computerised over the past 40 years are in areas of especially low payoff (Strassman 1990). Payrolls, ledgers and registers clearly fall into this area. Also too much time and attention has been spent perfecting the detail of such systems. Key business systems with real economic payoff have received relatively little attention.

The second argument is that information technology practices have been laid on top of existing manual practices and thus there has been no real economic gain for the firm. This argument says that if manual procedures are simply computerised then the best that may be achieved is direct cost displacement, i.e. people or other resources are taken out of the firm and computer technology costing about the same as the displaced people, is inserted. What is needed is for information technology to radically change the way various business processes are conducted. This is variously referred to as business reengineering, business process re-engineering, business re-configuring, business reshaping or business redesign. Thus, it is sometimes argued that only with the radical application of this technology will it be possible to generate real and substantial business benefits which will be clearly seen in the return on investment numbers.

4.5 The strategic information systems phenomenon

It would indeed be unfair to suggest that all organisations always suffer severe cases of the culture gap with all the information systems activities they undertake. In some instances the information systems people and line managers work very effectively together in close partnership. This is especially true where organisations develop strategic information systems. A strategic information system is also known as a competitive edge system and may be defined as:

> 'an information system which helps a firm improve its long term performance by achieving its corporate strategy and thereby directly increasing its value added contribution to the industry value chain.' (Remenyi, 1988)

These relatively new[4] types of information systems require the close collaboration of information systems staff, line managers and end users (McKeen and Smith 1996; Remenyi 1990; Wiseman 1985; Synnott 1987). They can deliver very real direct business benefits and their development opens up the scope of

---

[4] Strategic information systems may be traced back to the 1970s when organisations such as American Airlines and American Hospital Supplies reported that significant competitive advantages had been obtained from their technology. However it is correct to say that the incidence of strategic information systems delivering a true competitive advantage are still relatively rare.

information systems more than any other previous approach to computing by allowing the technology to actually play a central role in how the firm conducts its business.

The concept of information systems being able to assist the firm in achieving its corporate strategy was received with open arms by both information systems and the general business communities. Strategic information systems were perceived by some as the finding of the philosophers' stone or the golden fleece of the information management profession. However not all the information systems, even in these firms, were strategic and also the majority of organisations did not develop systems which were so mission critical that they required this high degree of collaboration or partnership between the three key business groups. Thus despite the considerable successes achieved by having a high degree of collaboration between information systems departments and other groups, there still remains a general problem in most organisations of bridging the so-called culture gap.

It is worth noting however, that those organisations who have had success with strategic information systems have, in many cases, followed a development approach which is not dissimilar to that suggested by ABR. At least in some respects these organisations had applied some of the notions inherent in post-modernism to information systems development.

5. POST-MODERN INFORMATION SYSTEMS MANAGEMENT

As discussed above, with increasing pressure for the information systems management to prove its efficiency and effectiveness, it is clear that the management of information systems is at an important cross-roads. The dissatisfaction with information systems management can be substantially alleviated by improving the return on investment using ABR which applies a number of basic notions derived from post-modern thinking and which imply that:

1. It is essential to have a meaningful and on-going evaluation of information systems and their benefits, clear understanding of those benefits by all stakeholders, and the commitment of all parties to the achievement of those benefits. Of course this implies the correct identification of the primary stakeholders and the effective co-evolution of information systems solutions to ensure ongoing commitment and success. There should be an appropriate concern for the use of language, especially the meaning and use of key words which are used to define the outcome.

2. It is necessary to deliver information system outcomes which keep pace with business change, include all relevant stakeholders and accept that there will be a shift in goals as the project proceeds. A focus on outcomes or direct business benefits is needed rather than systems or information system outputs.

3. It is important to realise that any proposed information systems solution is always contingent on the set of circumstances which are presently in operation and which in the current environment may quickly change. Thus considerable emphasis needs to be placed on flexibility and a mind-set which is welcoming to change this is facilitated by futuring which is addressed in some detail later in this chapter.

6. CO-CREATION AND CO-EVOLUTION OF SYSTEMS

At the heart of the success of the application of post-modern principles to information systems development is a positive attitude on the part of the eventual users towards their co-evolutionary role in systems development. This should be achieved through a disciplined continuous participative approach focusing on their ownership of the system and involving a sound relationship between the main stakeholders, i.e. the information systems personnel, financial staff, line managers and end users (Pyburn 1991). User ownership is a sine qua non for information systems success. The positive relationship between the stakeholders which is sometimes referred to as partnership will lead to the co-evolution of systems which is also central to information systems success.

6.1 Ownership

In order to understand the issue of systems ownership it is necessary to bear in mind the reason why information systems are implemented. Information systems are developed and implemented in order to deliver business benefits which will either improve the efficiency, the effectiveness or the strategic potential of the firm. It therefore follows that these systems should be owned by the individuals and/or departments who are attempting to improve their efficiency, effectiveness or strategic potential.

The systems ownership issue refers to ensuring that it is clearly understood who has responsibility for the information system and especially for its success. This is a wide ranging responsibility which includes identifying the system's opportunity, performing an ex-ante appraisal of the system's potential, managing the system's development, overseeing its commissioning and eventually performing a post-implementation audit.

Users are a critical source of information during the analysis and the design stages of the software development life cycle. During these stages the users' input has a profound influence on how the system will be developed and what sort of facilities it will offer. Issues, such as whether the systems will be on-line or real time, are most important considerations which need user involvement to resolve. By evaluating the proposal and influencing the design decisions a sense of ownership becomes developed by the users. This sort of experience is important to users for several reasons, including the fact that it makes the training of them much easier as they will already understand the basis around which the system is being developed.

Once the system has been commissioned it is then effectively transferred to the user or users and at this stage the information systems department will certainly play a lesser role, largely to do with maintenance. From this point onwards users regard their information systems as important business assets and the general principles of asset management should be applied to these investments. In this respect the portfolio theory for information systems developed by McFarlan (1984) is very useful.

It is also important that the users evaluate the success of the system. They should decide whether the investment money was well spent and whether further funds are required to develop the system to a more advanced stage.

It is not easy to achieve a sense of systems ownership among the users, and firms who regard this attitude as important have to expend a considerable amount of effort to ensure that it will happen and that the attitude of ownership will remain over the life of the system[5]. Ownership issues are a basic concern to

---

[5] In discussion with focus groups it is clear that systems ownership is a major cause of concern in many organisations. Line managers and eventual users sometimes try to off load their responsibility on to the information systems department. Sometimes line managers do not attend scheduled meetings to discuss requirements or they send very junior staff who cannot make an adequate contribution to the information systems requirement discussion and decision making (Berghout and Klompe 1996). It is not

commercially minded staff who see corporate financial performance as a critical issue.

6.2 Partnership

The relationships between the stakeholders need to be in the context of internal partnerships. Having a positive internal partnership means removing all the attitudes described by Robert Townsend (1984) and replacing them with positive working relationships. For most firms this means a fairly substantial change. In fact, a new co-operative paradigm is needed for the mid-1990s. And new paradigms of this magnitude require the backing and visible support of the most senior managers. This is supported and expanded upon by Selig (1991) when he says:

> 'Partnership relations ... will not emerge overnight, nor be established by edict. They must develop over time, through frequent interaction....'

Without this positive relationship, substantial waste in information technology resources is inevitable, if for no other reason than through misunderstandings. It is frequently misunderstandings which lead to delays in systems delivery and budgetary overspends. This partnership development will close the culture gap, and the principle of co-evolution of information systems is an important approach to this because it provides a basis of common interest to which all the sides can relate.

---

easy to solve such problems. One approach is to ensure that the commitment to the information system is at a high enough level in the organisation to inspire department or divisional heads to identify with its success. The way that this may be achieved is of course a function of the corporate culture, but whatever the culture it is seldom easy to achieve.

Despite the difficulties associated with partnership development it is clear that this approach is essential in order to obtain any degree of strategic benefits from an organisation's information systems.

7. BENEFIT IDENTIFICATION

The high level of criticism levelled at the information systems function has resulted in greater energy being directed towards finding ways and means of ensuring that information systems are seen to deliver suitable benefits. Some organisations have mastered this but others are still trying. There are problems of being aware of the types of benefits which can realistically be expected and this requires a much better understanding of what types of benefits can be achieved by the application of information systems. In turn an understanding of direct business outcomes resulting from information systems is necessary and this will be discussed in detail in a later chapter.

Of course even when information systems are delivered speedily and are relatively error free many organisations still do not reap the full business benefits of new systems application development. This was addressed by Raho *et al.* (1987) when they said:

> 'In spite of the strategic importance of keeping pace with technology advances, the ability of most businesses to assimilate and apply information technology lags far behind the available opportunities.'

And this according to Sankar (1991) is attributable not to technology issues but rather to organisational ones. This view is also supported by Lederer and Sethi (1992) and Ward *et al.* (1996).

8. FUTURING TO IMPLEMENT ORDERED CHANGE

Karl Albrecht (1994) observes that static organisations are shifting to chaotic organisations, and that the old cry of 'back to basics' is not only futile, but severely limiting to the chances of future success. He says that goals will constantly change and that successful businesses will move away from planning to 'futuring':

> 'Futuring should acknowledge the fact that hitting the exact targets of any plan you could write would be a sheer accident.'

Albrecht goes on to define a futuring method which concentrates on the defining of business outcomes, the gap analysis between the present situation and the desired future outcome, and the action planning and strategy deployment which is needed to close that gap.

Information systems which are not built with a futuring mind-set are likely to miss their target, which will probably have moved anyway. A possible answer to business futuring will be for information systems professionals to concentrate on defining the business outcomes, identifying changes in goals as the stakeholders become clearer on the outcome and tracking progress towards these outcomes. It will become important to identify changes in any of the parameters which were used to define the outcome, changes in the stakeholders and changes in the language which is used to describe the outcome. By communicating and agreeing these changes on an ongoing basis, it should be possible to constantly narrow the gap between the present state and the desired outcome. Both information systems professionals and management should accept that the necessary constant innovation required to achieve outcomes will also mean constantly changing goals, and with a change in mind-set, it is possible to manage within this environment.

9. FORMATIVE OR CONTINUOUS PARTICIPATIVE EVALUATION AT THE CENTRE OF POST-MODERNISM

As may be seen from the above discussions a central feature of post-modernism is the realisation of the fact that change is inevitable and complex. In order to be able to assess what type of change is required or how much change is needed regular monitoring of information systems development activities and the regular review of business objectives is essential. This centres on the evaluation of how information systems are being realised and how the business context is evolving.

In this context evaluation needs to be performed using a formative paradigm, as continuous participative evaluation which facilitates the process of change management. This evaluation needs to include an assessment of human needs and values. Summative evaluation which may also be useful is however not as important as formative which may be used to continuously re-direct the organisation through the process of co-evolution.

9.1 Traditional approaches to information systems evaluation

In general, the tools available for information systems evaluation and how accountants or managers calculate costs and benefits are not well understood by either line managers or information systems staff. The traditional approach has been summative and thus of only limited use from the point of view of information systems management. Furthermore many organisations do not perform evaluations or cost benefit analysis on their information systems at all, and those who do, sometimes report mixed or confused results.

9.2 A post-modern approach to evaluation

There is a growing understanding that the financial figures alone cannot represent a convincing picture of the role which information systems play in an organisation. In the first place there are numerous difficulties associated with being able to identify the appropriate costs, let alone the benefits of an information system. On the question of benefits there are both tangible and intangible benefits to be accounted for, and intangible benefits are by definition very difficult to quantify (Remenyi *et al.* 1995).

A post-modern understanding of evaluation involves the acceptance that evaluation is:

1. a management process requiring discipline;

2. comprehensive, involving the opinions of all the major stakeholders as informed project partners;

3. focused on a full range of benefits or outcomes which include financial and direct business benefits, both tangible and intangible;

4. most effective when it is performed regularly perhaps even continuously;

5. not critical of change but rather sympathetic to it, encouraging full discussion of co-evolving requirements;

6. required to ensure that the object or process being evaluated continues to be relevant.

If evaluation is used in this way it will lead to a much higher standard of information systems management. This will result in more successful information systems being developed in shorter time frames and providing opportunities whereby management can achieve a better outcome for their organisation.

10. SUMMARY AND CONCLUSION

There is a need for major changes in the way information systems are managed. This has been evidenced by continuous complaints about the lack of financial returns on the ever increasing investment in information systems. The traditional approach to information systems development is no longer valid as we reach the end of the twentieth century. There is a need to redefine how information systems contribute to the organisation and how they are to be managed. This is not surprising as management itself has not performed all that well over the past thirty years and is also in need of some substantial re-thinking.

The authors propose ABR as a different approach to information systems development which incorporates a post-modern perspective on the nature of business and management. In this chapter some of the post-modern thinking has been reviewed on a broad level and key aspects applied to information systems development and especially to issues relating to ensuring that information systems investment delivers an appropriate return on the funds committed.

This approach focuses on four primary issues which are:

1. The focus on outcomes rather than outputs, and the constant and disciplined tracking of outcome definitions over time through the process of continuous participative evaluation.

2. The management of relationships, partnering, co-creation, co-evolution and ownership issues.

3. All stakeholders are fully committed to the realisation of the benefit that will be derived from the attaining of the required outcome.

4. A development process which is sympathetic to the above relationship issues, and which acknowledges that the goal-posts *will* change.

Central to these factors playing a role in the establishment of a new information systems paradigm, is the acceptance that the goals in general and specific goal-posts will *and should* shift, and delivery and relationships must be managed within that mind-set.

To make information systems work effectively at the end of the 1990s, it is essential that the old culture gap problems with all the internal tension which accompanies it, and which was so well described by Townsend and corroborated by Grindley and others, be eradicated. This means that new attitudes of co-evolution need to be inculcated into IT professionals as well as other line and staff managers.

The above amounts to a major challenge for corporate management which requires a significant mind-set or culture change, both in how the information system department functions internally as well as how it works with other parts of the business. The authors believe that all this is generally within the capabilities of most information systems departments.

Unless information system functions embrace this post-modern thinking and become fast enablers of business change, become partners in attaining business outcomes, and facilitate the achievement of clearly understood benefits for the business, they may fall prey to the question that Gellerman (1990) proposes:

> 'Ask not: "How well is that unit performing its role?"
> but rather, "Is that role necessary or even desirable?"'

It is imperative that information systems managers and their senior colleagues accept the view expressed in A.A. Milne's (1926) classic, *Winnie-the-Pooh* by Edward Bear, coming downstairs, bump, bump, bump, on the back of his head, behind Christopher Robin, that there is another way – in their case of managing the information systems resource, if only they could stop bumping for a moment and think their way through to a more post-modern approach.

3

Some Aspects of Information Systems Evaluation

'But every future will someday be past: if we see the past truly now, it must, when it was still future, have been just what we now see it to be and what is now future must be just what we shall see it to be when it become past'.

Bertrand Russell, Mysticism and Logic, 1970.

1. INTRODUCTION

Evaluation has a key role to play in ensuring information systems success. This chapter and Chapter Four explicitly put evaluation in evidence as a management process in information systems development.

The apparent failure of some information systems investments to contribute to the business success is in part due to the inadequate recognition given to the business, social and human dimension of information systems investment programmes. Technical and financial issues have traditionally dominated this area at the expense of more general people and organisational considerations and this chapter considers some aspects of the evaluation of these issues.

Much of the theoretical foundation for organisational evaluation research is based on work conducted as part of the evaluation of educational and social programmes. Some aspects of evaluation theory for social programmes are appropriate for IS evaluation and these theories underpin, to some extent, the ABR approach to the evaluation of information systems.

This chapter discusses the concepts and some generic aspects of evaluation, which are then applied to the evaluation of information systems. The theoretical foundation is based on work by researchers such as Scriven (1991:a&b), House (1993), Walsham (1993), Finne *et al.* (1995), Rebien (1996) and a doctoral dissertation on evaluation written by Sherwood-Smith (1989).

2. WHAT IS EVALUATION?

Before discussing information systems evaluation it is worth considering the concept of evaluation in a broader context. The Shorter Oxford dictionary gives the following definition: 'the action of working out the value of something'. Evaluation is a weighing up process to assess the value of an object or the merit of a situation and it is on this basis that the definition used in this book is developed.

A more formal definition of evaluation would state that:

> Evaluation is a series of activities incorporating understanding, measurement and assessment. It is either a conscious or tacit process which aims to establish the value of or the contribution made by a particular situation. It can also relate to the determination of the worth of an object.

The evaluation proposed here is process[1] based and it directly supports management decision making and its primary objective is the maximisation of benefits potentially available from an information system's investment.

Winograd and Flores (1987) in their seminal book on computer systems design, *A New Foundation for Design*, succinctly define design as the interaction between understanding and creation. They state:

> '... we must open the question of design: the interaction between understanding and creation. In speaking here of design ... we address the broader question of how society engenders inventions whose existence in turn alters that society. We need to establish a theoretical basis for looking at what the devices do, not just how they work.'

In this chapter, evaluation is viewed with the same perspective mirroring the views expressed by Winograd and Flores. Thus the approach to evaluation in this chapter focuses on what the system does, its value to the business and organisational outcomes, and not on the technological merits of the system.

Evaluation is an interaction between understanding and measurement. So to evaluate anything the evaluator should first understand what he or she is evaluating. This aspect of understanding is reflected in Scriven's (1991:a) definition of

---

[1] A process is a series of structured activities, in this case of evaluation activities. The process starts at IS project initialisation. Each activity is clearly defined and logically and sequentially leads on to the next activity. In addition because of the highly structured nature and progression of these activities the process provides a rational and controlled means of project termination. Within this process there may be an iteration of certain of the activities.

evaluation cited by House (1993) in which he says that evaluation is:

> 'Usually defined as the determination of the worth or value of something … judged according to appropriate criteria, with those criteria explicated and justified.'

Not only does the evaluator have to understand what is being evaluated but he or she should clearly understand the norms by which the object or situation is being measured and assessed. To evaluate an information system it is necessary to understand what the organisation is attempting to achieve through the use of the information system, assess the organisational context, and then measure the value of the results of its use.

Evaluation is a process that is intuitively known or at least instinctively undertaken by everyone. It is either a conscious or instinctive reviewing process. Thus football teams, motor cars, the National Health Service, summer holidays as well as business investments are evaluated. In fact, Shadish *et al.* (1991) open Chapter One of their book by stating:

> 'We can evaluate anything including evaluation itself.'

There are many facets to evaluation and some of these are briefly highlighted in the following sections.

2.1 Purpose of evaluation

Allied to the definition of evaluation is the concept of the purpose of the evaluation exercise. This is reflected by Walsham (1993) who states that:

> 'A key element of the evaluation … is the purpose for which the evaluation is being carried out; this purpose may be explicitly stated or may be implicit…'

Evaluation is normally performed for a specific purpose which frequently leads on to some course of action. Legge (1984) argues that the primary function of all evaluations is to either sustain or to question the status quo. In the evaluation of social and development aid programmes the main purposes as seen by Rebien (1996) are to inform ongoing activities, to provide information and experience for designing and planning future activities and formulating policies.

Evaluation needs to be seen as a management device. In fact according to Love (1991):

> '... evaluation began to be recognised as an indispensable tool for managers and an essential part of the management process.'

Another issue is the gravity of the situation being evaluated. The assessment process usually reflects the significance and purpose of the ultimate application. For example, the evaluation required for the selection of which approach to use to tackle the morning's routine work requires little weighing up, whilst the evaluation required for the selection of a new information system requires significant weighing up. And the evaluation of an aid programme for a developing country is an even more serious undertaking. However, all involve the same essentials; an understanding of the problem domain and a 'weighing up' or measurement of the contribution of alternative courses of action against some objectives.

2.2 An interactive inquiring system

To be competent the evaluator should first understand what he or she is evaluating: its substance, its qualities. The evaluator should understand the context and evaluation method. Through this interaction value is assessed.

At the centre of the evaluation process is a management information system. Hopwood (1983) in his discussion on 'Evaluating the Real Benefits' of information technology points out that an evaluation is a complex information processing exercise:

> 'Be aware that the evaluation exercise is itself a complex information processing activity, subject to all the problems and opportunities which characterise this area.'

An evaluation exercise may be seen as an enactment of an inquiring system (Churchman 1971; Thompson 1967; Dumas 1978)[2], the purpose of which is to produce knowledge to support the assessment of the value of the object or the merit of the situation in order to make decisions.

The decision making process in evaluation, applied to a single aspect of an information system, is explained and illustrated in Figure 3.1, which is adapted from Thompson's model (1967).

In Figure 3.1 the decision making context is shown as a two by two matrix. The x axis represents the evaluators 'Level of Understanding' of the issue under consideration and the clarity of their beliefs about the cause and effect of any action which they propose. If the decision maker's level of understanding is complete, this implies confidence in their view of the impact of their decision. On the y axis the evaluators' level of certainty about the acceptability of this aspect of the information system

---

[2] An inquiring system is 'A system which produces knowledge'. A complete discussion can be read in Churchman's book (1971). The term is used here in the sense that to support the final act of evaluation it is necessary to produce knowledge about the substance and the qualities of the system to be evaluated and to produce knowledge about the measurement norms.

is shown[3]. On the diagram this is shown as 'Standard of desirability'.

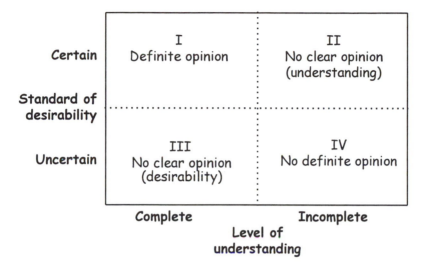

	I	:	II
Certain	Definite opinion	:	No clear opinion (understanding)

Figure 3.1: The decision making process in evaluation

Figure 3.1 illustrates a taxonomy of four situations in which evaluators may find themselves. In the type I quadrant the evaluator's understanding of that aspect of the system is complete and he or she is certain about the level of acceptability. This view may be that the outcome is acceptable or unacceptable, but the evaluator has a definite opinion. In the type II, III and IV quadrants the evaluator's level of understanding is incomplete, or there is uncertainty about the level of acceptability of the information system, or both. The objective of the process of evaluation is to bring everyone's decision making into the type I quadrant, where they have a definite opinion.

---

[3] On the original diagram proposed by Thompson the axes were: (*x*) The beliefs of the decision makers about the future outcomes, and (*y*) The standards of desirability against which the effects of causal action can be evaluated. The topic is discussed in Dumas (1978), pages 53 et seq.

The problem of decision making is compounded for the evaluation of an information system as there may be many aspects which need to be evaluated. This is represented in Figure 3.2. The previous diagram showed a single plane. For a whole system there are many decision making planes. These include organisational, operational and technological considerations and each of these is multivariate. Consequently for the information systems evaluator there are many decision making planes to consider[4].

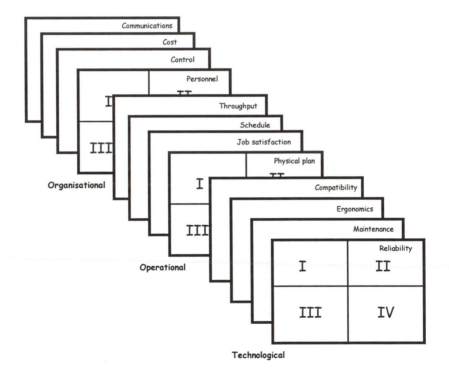

Figure 3.2: Multiple planes for evaluation

---

[4] Currently the actual evaluation criteria (planes and dimensions) are poorly understood and this further compounds the problem. The issue of evaluation criteria and what benefits to evaluate are considered later in this book.

Because there are multiple stakeholders and therefore evaluators, the first problem is to bring individual evaluators' decisions into the type I quadrant. This objective is not always reached for all participants in an evaluation. Some will have an incomplete knowledge of the effects of the information system, perhaps due to lack of time to study the system fully or lack of experience in information systems. Others may be uncertain about the acceptability of the system because by nature not all people are decisive and some evaluators will have ambivalent views about acceptability. Through discussion, negotiation, further analysis and education the evaluation process should at least bring evaluators towards type I conclusions by decision making time.

Having brought decisions to the type I quadrant for each plane, the next problem is to aggregate the decisions over all the planes to arrive at a single view. For a single evaluator this process of arriving at a single view can be seen as having achieved a holistic evaluation of the information system. However the evaluation of an information system, particularly in a participatory evaluation context will certainly involve many evaluators and consequently it is unlikely that participants in an evaluation will attempt to express a holistic evaluation. It is much more likely that they will express their view of the system in terms of it satisfying some criteria and falling short in others and so the evaluation process will be a discussion, clarification, assessment and negotiation process. Referring to the decision making model in Figure 3.2, all participants in an evaluation should negotiate towards using the same decision making planes.

A fundamental aspect of the evaluation system is clarification of and agreement on the important measurable properties of the information system to be evaluated. Once the evaluation criteria have been agreed, an individual evaluator assesses, according to his or her judgement, the value of the system against these norms. These individual views may then be pooled and through further negotiation a collective agreement on the course of action to be taken in the context of improving the value of the information system.

2.3 The time dimension to evaluation

The interactive evaluation process described above may be carried out intuitively in day to day life, or the interaction may take a day at a management meeting when evaluating and justifying the decision to go ahead on a particular IS project. On the other hand the evaluation may be a process of a series of assessment activities over a much longer period. So there is a time dimension to evaluation. Evaluations, which at a micro level can be viewed as a small interactive process, are carried out as acts of evaluation or can be viewed as an evaluation process. This is discussed in more detail in the section 'An evaluation process or an evaluation act' in Chapter Four.

2.4 People are central to evaluation

Evaluations are conducted by people. The evaluator may attempt to minimise the personal bias of the evaluation by using an objective method and objective data.

The traditional view of information systems evaluation sees the evaluation either as a feasibility study or as an audit (ex-post) or as a management evaluation. In contrast to this traditional view, ABR views information systems evaluation as participative. An evaluation act is a purposeful act, in the sense that the evaluator assesses the system in their terms, and for their purpose. This is identified by Walsham (1993) who states there are a 'multiplicity of private rationalities' which influence an evaluation.

Participative evaluation implies that a group is involved. The fundamentals of evaluation and all the complexities of individual interpretation of value persists for a group situation and often further complexity is added. Each individual group member's understanding of the information system will be different, the desirability of the system will be different and in a group situation the personal behaviour and stance of each individual member may influence the evaluation. A common understanding should be arrived at and then an agreed course of action negotiated.

3. TYPES OF EVALUATION

There are a number of taxonomies which allow the categorisation of evaluation techniques and methodologies. The following sections examine two of the primary categories of evaluation, which are ex-ante and ex-post evaluations and summative and formative evaluations.

3.1 Ex-ante and ex-post evaluation

Predictive evaluations performed to forecast and evaluate the impact of future situations are sometimes referred to as *ex-ante* evaluations. Post-implementation evaluations that assess the value of existing situations are sometimes referred to as *ex-post* evaluations. Ex-ante evaluations are normally performed using financial estimates which may be either single point estimates of costs and benefits or range estimates of such figures. In either case this type of analysis attempts to forecast the outcome of the information systems investment in terms of an indicator or set of indicators such as the payback, the net present value or the internal rate of return, to mention only three.

The purpose of ex-ante evaluation is to support systems justification. Systems justification, which is sometimes confused with evaluation, implies first an evaluation and then the activity of justification, showing that the information system is appropriate for the particular business context. The purpose of ex-post evaluation is to assess and confirm, or refute, the value of a realised design or a completed action. The ex-post or the post-implementation evaluations investigate and analyse the current system to examine 'what is' against some previously suggested situation. This is done to confirm the value of the system and support operational decisions about improvements. Ex-post evaluations may be made on the basis of financial indicators such as those described for the ex-ante situation above or they may be made using other non-financial measures such as user satisfaction surveys.

Ex-ante or predictive evaluations are complex. The evaluator has to understand the existing system in order to predict and understand the future system, as well as be able to estimate the potential impact of the future situation. On the other hand ex-ante evaluations only require estimates of likely costs and benefits while ex-post evaluation require actual costs and actual benefits which are sometimes very difficult to determine.

3.2 Formative and summative evaluation

Evaluation activities may also be categorised as *formative* and *summative*. Formative evaluation which is sometimes referred to as learning evaluation (Senge 1992) has been explained by Finne *et al.* (1995) as:

> '… Formative evaluation approaches typically aim at improving program performance, take place while the program is in operation, rely to a large extent on qualitative data and are responsive to the focusing needs of program owners and operators.'

This theme is expanded by Patton (1980) who points out:

'Formative evaluations are conducted for the purpose of improving programs in contrast to those evaluations which are done for the purpose of making basic decisions about whether or not the program is effective.'

The term formative is taken from the word *form*, 'to mould by discipline and education'. Formative evaluation is viewed as an iterative evaluation and decision making process continually influencing the social programme and influencing the participants, with the overall objective to achieve a more acceptable and beneficial outcome from the programme. Summative evaluation on the other hand, derived from the word *sum*, is viewed as an act of evaluation assessing the final (sum) impact of the social programme. Adelman (1996) points out that summative and formative are conditions of the evaluator in contrast to process and product, which are conditions of the evaluation.

It is recognised that in systems design both formative and summative evaluation takes place. Hewett (1986) describes this:

'As applied to development of computer systems, formative evaluation involves monitoring the process and products of system development and gathering user feedback for use in the refinement and further system development. Summative evaluation involves assessing the impact, usability and effectiveness of the system; the overall performance of user and system.'

Hewett goes on to point out that in systems development these two types of evaluation are required in mixes of different proportions at different stages in the development cycle. In practice there is an overlap of the two conditions. The adoption of either summative or formative evaluation approaches depends on the preferences and needs of those performing the evaluation of the information system.

An example of this overlap is the FAOR[5] benefits analysis framework for IS evaluation which recognises four types of evaluation study (Schaefer 1988), An *Exploration Study*, A *Planning Study*, A *Decision Study*, A *Control Study*. These four types of evaluation do not fall neatly into either the formative or summative taxonomy. The first three might be termed formative in that they support the design process and the control study is clearly a summative evaluation. However, the exploration study may also be termed summative as it evaluates reality to initiate some new development.

Formative evaluation is not only about measuring the contribution, but also about the inclusion of the views of a wide range of the stakeholders. It does not stop at summary statistics, but probes the reality behind the numbers in order to understand what is really going on, i.e. what is being achieved, what is to be achieved and what the current and potential problems are. Adelman (1996) suggests:

> '... that formative admits more representational equity than summative and giving equal voice to all stakeholders also admits diversity.'

The terms formative and summative do not in themselves imply participation for formative evaluation and non-participation for summative evaluation. From its definition 'moulding by discipline and education' there is at least an expectation that stakeholders are involved in a formative evaluation process. But

---

[5] The FAOR project (Functional Analysis of Office Requirements) is a European funded project in the Esprit programme. The project has produced an approach to office requirements analysis. Part of this approach, the Benefits Analysis Framework, is directly relevant to evaluation.

it is also clear that a participatory summative evaluation can take place.

3.3 Participatory evaluation

Rebien (1996) in his paper on participatory evaluation sets out to present a theoretical strengthening of the participatory evaluation concept. His paper is written in the context of the evaluation of development assistance programmes. Many of the concepts which he has clearly summarised in his paper are appropriate for information systems evaluation. Some of these are highlighted to support the premise and belief that information systems evaluation should be participatory evaluation.

Brunner and Guzman (1989) make the following claim for participatory evaluation.

'Participatory evaluation is an educational process through which the social groups produce action-oriented knowledge about their reality, clarify and articulate their norms and values, and reach a consensus about future action.'

The question of the degree of participation in an evaluation is also raised by Rebien as being a problem. Participation ranges from what might be termed genuine participation, in which the stakeholders are both the objects and subjects of the evaluation, to token participation or no participation at all. In a genuinely participative environment the opinions of the users are seriously treated and power-sharing in the evaluation occurs. Rebien concludes the discussion on participation by pointing out that:

'the conceptual weakness of participation implies that there is also a conceptual weakness in relation to participatory evaluation ... Who should participate?

What degree of stakeholder involvement constitutes participation?'

He also raises the question of the relative resources and negotiating power of the various stakeholders.

In the context of information systems development, the problem of who should participate can be solved. First, the context for an information systems development programme is much more restricted than for a social programme and, secondly, if the objectives of the introduction of a new information system in terms of desired business outcomes and targeted business benefits is clearly stated, then the stakeholders who have an interest in the benefits or are unfavourably affected by the consequence of the benefits can be identified[6].

The conceptual weakness of participatory evaluation with respect to the degree of organisational power of the stakeholders still remains even when the appropriate stakeholders have been found for an IS development programme. Evaluations can be manipulated and it is likely in this case, when there is no will or mind-set to participate, that information systems success will be limited. This falls back into what is happening at present.

Rebien's paper goes on to discuss fourth-generation evaluation defined as:

'an interpretative approach to evaluation based on and guided by issues identified by stakeholders.'

He lists the advantages of this approach from Guba and Lincoln (1989) which all support the premise that to close the evaluation

---

[6] The clarity of the definition of the objectives for the information system is a critical success factor for the systems development programme. This is discussed in Chapters Eight and Nine, which also describe the technique of the stakeholders/benefit matrix which identifies anomalous stakeholders.

gap in information systems evaluation, stakeholders must be involved.

Another important characteristic of participatory evaluation is that it is context bound. Because participatory evaluation is purposeful and depends on the people involved, the particular problem and context, the result cannot be generalised. Information systems evaluation is by nature context bound. Every organisational system is different because it depends on people. Failure to recognise this has resulted in many information systems failures. Technological solutions (and these can be normalised) have to be embedded in a unique business and organisational environment, which means that the evaluation of the whole systems operation, i.e. the evaluation of the outcomes should be participative.

4. SUMMARY AND CONCLUSION

Evaluation is people dependent and evaluations are purposeful acts which are context dependent and subject to the evaluator's purpose, needs and aspirations during the evaluation.

ABR is concerned with evaluation to support decision making in information systems development. To work out the value of a system the evaluator, through an interactive process, should ideally be guided into a position where he or she has a full understanding of the situation and a definite opinion about the value of the system. In information systems evaluation there are many aspects of the system that have to be evaluated and the evaluator should be prepared to aggregate his or her opinions about the various aspects of the system. Evaluation for an information system is not a single act of evaluation but is usually an evaluation process spread over a long period.

Evaluations can be categorised as ex-ante and ex-post. Ex-ante being evaluations before the realisation of the activity being evaluated to predict the outcome of the activity. Ex-post are after the event evaluations assessing the merit of what has been achieved. Evaluation can also be categorised as formative or summative. Evaluators in a formative evaluation are in the frame of mind to learn from the evaluation exercise to improve the performance of the activity, programme or system being evaluated, whilst evaluators performing a summative evaluation are only concerned with assessing merit of the finality of an action, programme or system.

Participatory evaluation explicitly includes the participation of a group of people in an evaluation with all the problems, diversity and opportunity which group participation entails. Participation is beneficial in that the participants learn and clarify their understanding of the programme or system being evaluated. If agreement is reached on various issues the participants are more likely to identify with the goals of the agreed actions and will be better motivated to realise the agreed objectives. Successfully managing participative evaluation needs disciplined management attention. The ABR approach is designed to give management this support so that participating stakeholders can benefit from the above advantages of a participative process.

4

Evaluation in the Management of IS Development

'If all economists were laid end to end, they would not reach a conclusion'

Attributed to George Bernard Shaw (1856–1950).

1. INTRODUCTION

Evaluation is an integral part of management. Intuitive or explicit evaluations are made to support management decisions throughout the development of an information system. Traditionally evaluation has been given little importance in the management of information systems development. The driving concern has always been the delivering of the components to build the technological system. This has led to the emphasis on project management in IS, systems analysis and design methods and computer programming methods. Less energy has been devoted to the quality and value of the information system or its appropriateness to supporting the business function.

This chapter describes the use of evaluation in information systems management, looks at some of the techniques that have been used for IS evaluation and goes on to place evaluation in the context of the information systems development life cycle.

It concludes by proposing a more formalised and better recognised role for evaluation prior to decision making in IS development.

2. EVALUATION AND MANAGEMENT

Evaluation is a central issue in society, especially within Western capitalist societies and has become an intrinsic part of the way in which humans conduct their lives. House (1993) states:

> 'The emergence of evaluation as a formal practice is a result of advanced capitalism.'

In recent years, evaluation has been associated with managerialism in an attempt to improve economic productivity and management (House 1993). In the business environment evaluation is at the heart of economic activity. One of the fundamental paradigms of modern economies is that capital markets are efficient and thus correctly allocate resources to areas which will improve or heighten performance and formal evaluation procedures have been developed to measure this.

In the 1950s and 1960s computers were purchased primarily as labour saving devices which essentially automated routine and repetitive tasks. For example, a payroll was automated with a computer-based process and a certain number of payroll clerks were made redundant or reassigned. During this period it was generally felt that the benefits of computing were self evident. In the 1970s to mid-1980s computers were recognised as having an impact on business effectiveness, these systems facilitated more effective management and control of organisations. During this era of computing the minimal investment in computer systems evaluation may be attributed to managers' reluctance to be involved in what they regarded as a technical area which could only be understood by highly qualified computer staff.

In the past decade there has been an increased awareness that information systems can radically transform the way in which organisations do business, transforming the established business practices and transforming the work environment for the organisation's staff.

Information systems are not seen as simply a tool to record transactions and process data, but as a competitive weapon which can change an industry structure, alter key competitive forces, and effect an organisation's choice of strategy (McFarlan 1990; Blanton *et al.* 1992; Cash and Konsynski 1995; Henderson and Treacy 1986; Johnston and Carrico 1988; Remenyi *et al.* 1995; Heafield 1995). As a result there is growing concern among both IS and business professionals as to whether the benefits of computing are being realised and thus the need for increased investment in IS evaluation.

Despite this increased role of Information Technology in organisations and increased expenditure there is considerable doubt as to whether IT investments are proving to be justifiable. Establishing or measuring the business value of computer-based systems have perplexed managers and researchers for several years (Hitt and Brynjolfsson 1994). A number of studies present contradictory evidence as to whether the expected benefits of computers have materialised (Attewell 1993; Brynjolfsson 1993; Wilson 1993; Hitt and Brynjolfsson 1994).

Many thus feel that IS evaluation has become a key management issue (Boyton and Zmud 1987; Kumar 1990; Silk 1990; Niederman *et al.* 1991; Earl 1992; Premkumar and King 1994; Kettinger and Lee 1995).

Despite this obvious need for evaluation, there is little agreement, among IS professionals and academics, as to specifically how the contribution of an information system to an organisation can be evaluated. Many instruments have been developed over the years to reliably measure IS efficiency and effectiveness. However at present there seems to be little consensus among researchers and practitioners as to which instrument or methodology is appropriate for IS evaluation.

3. EVALUATION AND INFORMATION SYSTEMS

A functional view of an information system is taken in this book. An information system consists of two co-operating systems a 'people work system' and a 'technological system'. This is illustrated below in Figure 4.1. The people work system consists of an organisation of people and an organisation of tasks. The technological system is a means of storing and communicating information to support the people in their organised tasks. The whole supports the business activity.

Information systems investments need to be evaluated for a number of reasons, which may be divided into two main categories related to operational issues. The first category is to do with the assessment of how well the organisation's funds or financial resources are being used, and the second category relates to how information systems evaluation can assist in the better management of the investment. Besides the operational aspect of information systems evaluation there is also the question of being able to satisfy top management of the strategic value of information systems.

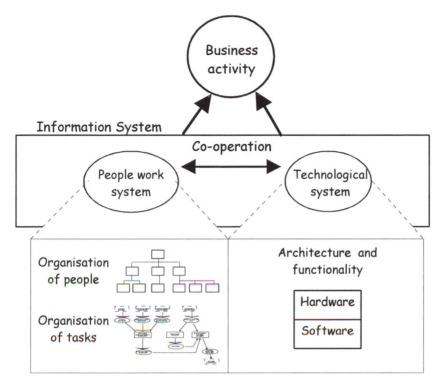

Figure 4.1: An information system

The main issue related to the utilisation of financial resources within the information systems environment is how to evaluate the contribution that a new information systems situation makes over the previous situation. And the key problem in the above situation is how to measure holistically the contribution made by the information system.

Evaluation is also a key strategy by which the management of information systems investments may be improved. There are two aspects to this. The first is to learn ex-post how the management may be improved in the future. The second is to support management decision making during the development and day to day running of an information systems operation to realise a better contribution from that investment.

The issues concerning the strategic value of evaluation to supporting management in information systems projects to deliver optimised business benefits are of particular interest to us in this book. The problem is not only how to measure holistically the contribution of an information system, but a compounding of this problem with the problems of what the evaluation process should be; who should be involved; how economically (with low cost, low effort and quickly) to represent the value of the contribution of the information system in an easy to understand way; how to arbitrate between conflicting evaluations and how to agree the course of action which delivers optimised benefits.

3.1 Summative evaluation in information systems

The majority of the studies and instruments for evaluating information systems, referenced earlier, have been concerned with this success of the information system and have been primarily summative in nature. Finne *et al.* (1995) suggest that such summative evaluations may be used conceptually, instrumentally, or persuasively. This means that the results of the evaluation may be used to reconsider an investment proposal, to redirect investment efforts or to convince others that a new course of action is required. In evaluating the success of the information system each of the above studies have considered a different type of measurement tool. Each of these measurement tools have considered different contingency variables such as organisational strategy, structure, size of the organisation, and individual characteristics of the system under investigation. No single instrument has been universally accepted as providing a valid and reliable summative measure of the information system being evaluated.

Summative evaluation which frequently is only performed once (Love 1991) is not appropriate for the purposes of improving the management of an investment. This is not only because summative evaluation is normally not reiterative, but also because it will usually focus on financial or other operating statistics and will not investigate in any detail the many issues which lie behind the numbers.

3.2　Formative evaluation in information systems

Hewett (1986) recognised that in information systems development there is an implicit formative evaluation activity. In information systems development the process of systems analysis and design has always included a formative evaluation facet, although it is seldom if ever referred to by that name. The systems analyst's dialogue with the user is a formative process. The systems design activity between computer specialist, analyst and user is a formative process, they formatively evaluate the proposed designs iteratively. The formative evaluation process is further influenced by the objectives of the information systems development project. They were given terms of reference and systems objectives, and part of the formative evaluation process for all of them is to understand these terms of reference and systems objectives and then to evaluate their progress and design in the context of these objectives.

In traditional approaches to information systems development formative evaluation has not been formalised as an evaluation process. As pointed out earlier, formative is a condition of the evaluator and certainly in information systems development the systems developer or the development team have had a formative frame of mind. The participation in the learning process has tended to be restricted to a small project team usually of technical staff and some selected line staff. Evaluations of a summative nature, which assess the total impact of the systems design, took place infrequently and it was only at these evaluations that the business benefits of the information systems investment were seriously considered. Furthermore a different set of people were involved in these summative evaluations, mostly management. The evaluation process tended to be primarily focused on cost and the objective was not to learn but more to command.

Figure 4.2 is a conceptual representation and description of formative evaluation as it is proposed in this book for information systems evaluation. It is represented as a process, a sequence of evaluation activities.

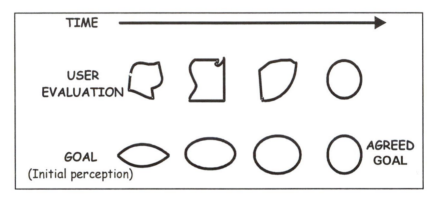

Figure 4.2: A formative evaluation process

As may be seen from the diagram, the formative evaluation process has three key characteristics. The first is the frequency of the evaluation. It is suggested that formative evaluation (applied correctly) is a frequent, if not quasi-continuous process.

The second characteristic is that an evaluator's perception of what is being evaluated changes and the value put on his/her perceptions changes as he/she learns more about the evaluation situation. Perceptions will be influenced as the evaluator's understanding of the business objectives and business requirements improve, and as their framework of values matures. Consequently an evaluation will evolve. This is known as the single-loop learning[1] aspect of the proposed formative evaluation process. The goals expressed as a rugby ball stay fixed but the evaluator's understanding evolves through the single-loop learning process.

The third characteristic is that the business situation changes over the life of a development project, the objectives of the information system will evolve during the formative evaluation process. Not only will the design be moulded by the formative evaluation process, but even the purpose of the information system investment may evolve. This is identified as the double-loop learning aspect of the proposed formative evaluation process. The basic business objectives which are driving the IS investment are challenged and changed if necessary in this double-loop learning process.

Using the analogy of a ball, Figure 4.2 illustrates four steps of a continuous process of formative evaluation. The initial management objective is to play rugby. The participants in the evaluation try to understand this and make a poor stab at it. In so doing they suggest that it is something like rugby that they would like to play, but they do not fully understand what is involved in the game especially with regard to the shape of a rugby ball. After the first round of discussions there is still significant discrepancy between the participants' understanding.

During a second discussion the participants debate what the real requirements are and in so doing slightly change their original positions. This continues during further formative evaluation sessions with the participants in the evaluation agreeing that it is a different game which is required with a slightly rounder ball.

---

[1] Single loop learning process evaluates the IS design and work in progress in the context of the goals and assumptions originally stated. The double loop learning process questions the assumptions and original goals as part of the formative process. Taken from Argyris and Schon (1978).

The process continues, with the evaluators understanding better and suggesting further modifications. And as can be seen in Figure 4.2 they all finally agree that association football meets the requirements.

Implied in the above description of the formative evaluation process is that it is a participatory evaluation process.

3.3 An evaluation process or an evaluation act

The predictive and post-implementation categorisation of evaluation focuses on when an evaluation takes place and is appropriate when evaluating the design and construction of an object or, as in this case, when evaluating the development of an information system. The categorisation is meaningful in the context of justifying a project or evaluating a project result. The summative and formative categorisation has not been generally used in the context of information systems design projects but these are quite appropriate conditions for information systems evaluators. Post-implementation evaluations are all perceived as summative evaluations. However, the term summative is rarely used to describe a 'one off' predictive evaluation, a systems justification exercise. A systems justification based on a predictive evaluation to assess the impact of the whole of an information system, is summative in nature. It evaluates the sum of the impact predictively. Summative evaluations are very much acts of evaluation be they predictive or post-implementation. Formative evaluation in information systems development, on the other hand, is a process.

So there is possibly a need for a further categorisation between acts of evaluation, be they ex-ante or ex-post, and an evaluation process to understand information systems evaluation. The Shorter Oxford English Dictionary defines a process as:

'... A continuous and regular action or succession of actions, taking place or carried on in a definite manner, a continuous (natural or artificial) operation or series of operations ... A particular method of operation ...'

In the business environment Davenport (1993) defines a process as:

'A process is simply a structured, a measured set of activities designed to produce a specified output for a particular customer or market.'

During information systems development an informal evaluation process continually guides the designer towards a systems design, with formal evaluation acts being made at the major decision making points in the development cycle. This second type of evaluation is formative in its objective, in that it supports the improvement of the design, but also summative in nature, as it is a milestone evaluation, assessing the work of a development stage and the potential impact of the information system if development is to proceed. So systems development is characterised by an informal formative process and by acts of evaluation, bursts of what is termed summative evaluation activity. Summative evaluation is a necessary preparatory activity to decision making at agreed milestones in the development cycle. These bursts of evaluation activity culminate in single decision making events about the progress of systems development. Decisions are made about major issues concerning the information systems design, the direction and the continuation of the systems development.

4. EVALUATION IN THE SYSTEMS DEVELOPMENT LIFE CYCLE

The exact pattern of the different evaluation activities applied will vary from one design methodology to another. It should also be understood that these activities are interdependent and should be using common information. Another point to note is that implicit in the definition of formative evaluation is the concept of participation. Without participation the formative aspect is very weak or non-existent.

The waterfall model of information systems development provides a classic example of utilising the different evaluation activities in an interdependent and interrelated manner. The formative evaluation process is not usually formalised in traditional information systems development and so the formative evaluation influence is weak. Figure 4.3 illustrates the waterfall model for systems development showing the utilisation of different evaluation methods.

Formative evaluation and tactical decision making takes place at each stage in the development cycle, but this is not formalised. It is less emphasised in the implementation phase because in the waterfall model of development the design phase will have crystallised the design and the specification phase concretises the system.

Summative evaluations take place at decision making points in the development cycle. In current management practice these have tended to be management decisions which involve the preparation and reading of reports (evidence collection), the calling of a meeting for an agreed group of participants (implicitly the 'one off' evaluation method) and a decision making meeting at which the system is presented, discussed and a decision made on how to proceed.

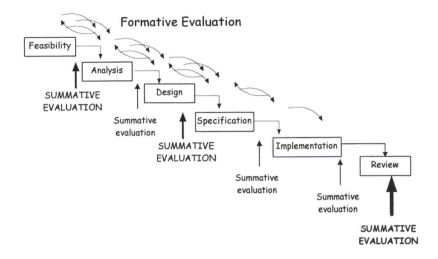

Figure 4.3: Traditional waterfall model with evaluation included

In the waterfall approach to systems development, which is largely discredited, the formative evaluation aspect has been very weak. Formative evaluation has been the privilege of a small technological design group, focusing on the analysis and design phases. The management and users have not been involved.

It has been recognised that systems design should be a more iterative process. Hewett (1986) emphasises the role of iterative evaluation in designing systems for usability:

'Just as the system changes with each evaluation-design iteration, so too the nature or goals of system evaluation can change with each evaluation-design iteration. Another reason for treating the evaluation process as an iterative process is that evaluation procedures themselves often need to be designed, and redesigned.'

The value of an iterative approach to information systems design has been recognised by the systems development community who are now moving towards prototyping and incremental delivery process models for systems development. These imply the evaluation of the design by users and the evaluation of risk by management at more regular intervals. This is illustrated in Figure 4.4 and is the direction pursued in this book. The evaluation activity should be more participative and directly aimed at the learning process so that what is 'learnt' at each step in the process can be carried forward into the overall development process.

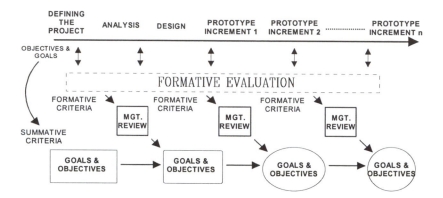

Figure 4.4: The proposed evaluation process in IS development

The evaluation starts at project definition when the goals and objectives are first set and continues through the development project which is illustrated in Figure 4.4 as an incremental delivery process. Formative evaluation is a continuous and sometimes informal process which continues throughout the development, influencing the process of development and the ultimate information system. Figure 4.4 also illustrates a series of formal management reviews which could take place at any time, but are seen as scheduled activities. These management reviews, which may be seen as being somewhat summative in nature, are participatory evaluations which take on board the more formal opinions of the stakeholders in the development project which may influence the goals and objectives which are shown as evolving over the project life. The evaluation activity should be more formalised than in the traditional approach so that what is learnt at each step in the process can be integrated into future activities in the project. A particularly important aspect of this approach is the acceptance that the information systems project can change over time. The bottom line of Figure 4.4 shows the evolutionary change of the goals and objectives throughout the course of the project. On the left side of the figure they are portrayed in a rectangle whereas on the right side of the figure they are shown in a circle. This suggests the possibility of substantial alterations to the project requirements between the time it is originally specified and when it is ultimately delivered.

In ABR information systems evaluation is based on a formative or learning evaluation paradigm, it is a formative evaluation process integrating some acts of evaluation. The process has as its primary objective the maximisation of benefits potentially available due to an information systems investment and in so doing adding value to the organisation as a whole. These evaluations should be seen as consumer-oriented evaluations as opposed to command-oriented evaluations. Each activity is clearly defined and logically and sequentially leads on to the next activity. Each activity is viewed as one in a series of activities which in totality make a holistic learning picture. In addition because of the highly structured nature and progression of these activities the process provides a rational and controlled means of realising project goals.

5. OWNERSHIP OF THE EVALUATION PROCESS

The identification of stakeholders and then agreeing who should participate can be a contentious problem. The identification of the stakeholders can be done systematically by establishing who benefits from or is affected by the information system.

The rationale for user participation in systems design is well established. It was first brought to prominence by Mumford (1983) in her book on the ETHICS (Effective Technical and Human Implementation of Computer-based Systems) method:

> 'Experience has shown that user involvement, clear job satisfaction objectives and a recognition of organisational factors will greatly assist the successful planning, design and implementation of computer-based work systems.'

The idea of participation has been more recently emphasised by Walsham (1993) who suggests that it is essential to information systems development because:

> 'The participation of users and other stakeholder groups in the design and development process can be considered as essential ...'

Participation is not always wholeheartedly subscribed to in the practice of business information systems development. The arguments are clear but the realisation of participation is exacting and demands particular management skills. Davenport (1993) identifies human resources as an enabler of process innovation, the radical, imaginative and IT enabled re-organisation of business or administrative processes. He warns of a need for a tough-minded and sensitive leader to realise success. The management of the development of information systems can readily be equated to the management of a process innovation project. The implication is that for a successful outcome the leadership must subscribe to a participative ethos. In 'Total Quality Management' approaches (TQM), bottom up contribution is encouraged and valued. It is a frame of mind *for participation* among stakeholders which is necessary for information systems evaluation if the system is to realise benefits for those stakeholders, who by definition are the business or its proxies. Morley (1993) in her paper on user participation confirms the difficulty of participation in the development in practice. She points to a lack of methodological support for participation as one of the problems. It is beyond the scope of this book to give a complete researched analysis and rationale for user participation, but it is implied that a participation by stakeholders is essential to information systems evaluation.

The type of mind-set that is needed is one in which the participants in the evaluation of the information systems are seen as enablers of and stakeholders in benefit realisation and the management of benefit realisation must be, as pointed out by Davenport (1993),

> 'consciously managing behavioural as well as structural change, with both a sensitivity to employee attitudes and perceptions, and a tough minded concern for results.'

Various reasons for participation are put forward ranging from a management's, sometimes half-hearted, attempt to implement a more democratic style of management, to a Union's wish to represent their members, to the information workers' wish to protect their personal interests. Mumford (1983) summarises this well:

> 'The challenge for any organisation that decides to try participation as a strategy is to create the kinds of structures and processes that will assist all the different stakeholders to obtain some gains from using this approach.'

Irrespective of the politics of user participation, on practical grounds the design and evaluation of an information system should be stakeholder driven. Whether it supports the business activity must be evaluated by management. Whether it is acceptable to operate, whether it is easily usable and whether it contributes to their job satisfaction must be evaluated by the operational and user staff. All these aspects can only be evaluated by users (management and staff) through their participation in the evaluation process.

The rationale for user participation is clearly supported and summarised by Adair (1985), and although stated over ten years ago its importance is still clear today.

> 'To summarise, most organisations today are people businesses. If nothing else, people are one of their biggest costs. It is essential for enterprises to create within themselves an environment or climate which really stimulates people to use their brains to a maximum. Leadership and good communications are therefore necessary to create those conditions. Then people will produce better corporate decisions, a higher standard of problem solving and much more creative thinking and innovation. Work will be more fun too.'

This does not imply that management surrender their responsibility. Management is responsible for providing leadership and making strategic decisions; however, users should participate in the evaluation and decision making which relates directly to the information systems which they utilise.

An adequate balance of management representation in terms of time and systems knowledge, and information worker representation in terms of influence is rarely seen (Mumford and Henshall 1979; Morley 1993). The composition of the evaluation and design teams should reflect the characteristics of the business problem to be solved and the complexity of the proposed information system. The ownership of the evaluation process must also reflect the above.

Allied to the question of participation is the question of the politics and ethics of evaluation. A problem identified by Walsham (1993) and Rebien (1996) is that user participation may be viewed as manipulative. For political reasons the perception of participation may be given to an evaluation process although the process is not genuinely participative. Users are invited to participate in what is termed a participative exercise but their participation is just for show and there is no genuine commitment to taking on board their evaluation of the information system. Another political aspect of participation in the evaluation exercise is power seeking, so that the participant in the evaluation takes a stance which influences his or her control on the information system or its outcomes. The converse of this would be the participant who would like to block the development of an information system. Participatory evaluation will take place in the current organisational structure and the current politics and these will ultimately determine the fate of the evaluation recommendations. ABR is based on the premise that if the business benefit is clearly identified and participants have a stake in the benefit and the business leadership is such that the organisation as a whole identifies with the benefit then the evaluation process will not be subject to political distortion. One of the advantages of having a well identified evaluation process is that these issues are brought into the open and are more likely to be resolved.

Another aspect of the politics of evaluation, not directly associated with user participation but nevertheless people related is what Walsham (1993) terms ritualistic evaluation in which an evaluation is carried out for form rather than for substance. These evaluations are management devices aimed at reassurance and security but not aimed at genuinely evaluating the information system with the view to take some positive action to improve the situation.

6. STAKEHOLDER NEGOTIATION

The implication of stakeholder participative evaluation of an information system is that the culminating steps of the evaluation are first a negotiation, based on individual opinions and stances in the evaluation situation, and this is followed by an agreement on some course of action to be taken. This process is illustrated in Figure 4.5. 'Participatory evaluation' implies an 'interpretatist evaluation' by individuals, this in turn implies a 'non-neutral evaluation' by individuals. However, the final step is a meeting of minds of the participant group, which offers self-validation, for the stakeholder group, through negotiation. The group collectively self-validates the individual evaluations.

Figure 4.5: Evaluation validated through negotiation

So participatory evaluation which produces a non-neutral evaluation result from the individuals involved is to a certain extent self-validated through a negotiation activity among the participants. This does not turn the process, de facto, into an objective evaluation but through negotiation the interpretatist bias is neutralised. The whole process can be viewed as a user negotiation. Throughout the evaluation the development team have participated in the formative process influencing the development of the information system. This is the groundwork for the more formal management reviews. At the key decision making points stakeholders negotiate and agree future courses of action. The value of the information system being designed is continually negotiated and agreed. The system is being designed to maximise its value through the decisions that are being made. This process will ensure an agreed design and a design that is of value to the negotiators.

This view of the evaluation process as a negotiation is mirrored by Walsham (1993) who refers to the process of IS evaluation as:

> '... a discourse, that is often mediated by formal techniques and procedures ...'

In participatory evaluation situations the interaction and negotiation process may be complex. The information gathered throughout the evaluation process will be quite extensive. Formal techniques and instruments to support the presentation of information to support evaluation and to support the negotiation will make the process more efficient and the whole evaluation more effective. This is briefly discussed at the end of this chapter.

Participatory evaluation in the information systems development context is primarily a social process and consequently the evaluation and negotiation may be antagonistic and confrontational. However, if it has reached this stage it is unlikely that the information system will realise business benefits and as has been pointed out earlier the advantage of having a methodical approach to evaluation is that these questions are confronted at an early stage in the development process.

7. EVALUATION AT THE HEART OF IS DEVELOPMENT

ABR is designed on the premise that the essential characteristics of the evaluation process in information systems development are: the integration of the evaluation process with a systematic design process, the focus on business benefits, a participatory evaluation process based on the formative evaluation paradigm, an iterative process interspersed with regular more formal evaluation acts. These are highlighted below.

7.1 A systematic approach

Evaluation must be approached in a systematic way. The evaluation process can be viewed as a management information system which assists in directing and controlling the development and operation of an information system. Both the process of evaluation and the information used in evaluation have to be controlled and managed. The process must be formalised so that a prescribed sequence of operations are followed to achieve an evaluation. Records have to be kept so that the information gathered during evaluation is not lost. Evaluation is an iterative process in which information is slowly accumulated and updated and this must be done in a controlled environment to allow a progression in the process. As an evaluator follows the process, his or her interpretation of the value of the information system evolves. This influences the course of the evaluation, which in turn affects the interpretation of the value of the final product. Every care should be taken to follow a systematic approach.

7.2 A problem oriented approach

To realise business benefits an information system is evaluated in the context of the unique goals and needs of a specific business situation. The evaluation process is problem oriented. No two information systems are identical. Different organisations may use the same hardware and software to satisfy the technological systems needs, but the way in which people use them and the needs they answer are individual to each situation. An information system may be implemented to meet a specific need or to resolve a particular problem. The evaluation of the system should thus be problem oriented in that it should focus on evaluating whether the proposed system resolves the business problem or creates the business opportunity.

7.3 A participatory approach

An information system is a tool in the hands of the users of the information system. The information system supports them in the execution of their business activity to realise business goals. These users are managers, operational managers, departmental staff and technical support staff. These are the stakeholders in the information system as an operational entity. These stakeholders should own the evaluation process so that value for them, in an agreed and balanced way, is built into the system and so that they are committed to what they have helped to develop for themselves.

7.4 A formative evaluation process

The evaluation paradigm is a formative one and the evaluation process is an iterative process. An information system is a complex system which cannot be appreciated by the evaluator in a one off exercise. Evaluators need to clarify their understanding of the system by iteratively refining their understanding. IS evaluation involves an educational and learning process.

The formative evaluation activity is an iterative evaluation-design activity. The knowledge gained through the evaluation is incrementally updated, causing the evaluator's judgement of the information system to evolve during the design process, during the system's implementation and during its operation.

7.5 Milestones

Evaluations at decision making points control the progress of information systems development at macro level to ensure that the major business, financial and scheduling objectives are being met. These are part of the whole systems evaluation process. They should be participative evaluation acts and the openness of a formative attitude should exist among all participants.

The evaluation process is both a refinement and incremental structuring process. The refinement of details can be achieved by iterative investigation, analysis and evaluation. The incremental structuring process of the evaluation is an evolving process. Information is gathered and the stored information is continually added to and updated. During all phases of participatory evaluation, evaluation criteria change and participants' perspectives change.

8. EVALUATION INSTRUMENTS

Users need effective and acceptable evaluation instruments to support the systematic evaluation process. The problem of effective user participation cannot be solved by declaring that evaluation and design should be user participative. Evaluation needs to be made easy for the participants. It is sometimes argued that user participation lengthens the information systems development process and increases the education effort and this is certainly true if no effort is made to support the participants in the development process. A manager or a departmental supervisor has not the time or possibly the inclination to get involved in the intricacies of systems design outputs or complex evaluation reports. Therefore the approach should be simplified to make evaluation more tractable. This can be achieved through clearly understandable benefits modelling systems and by giving users appropriate evaluation instruments to work with. It is beyond the scope of this book to fully discuss what instruments are available and appropriate for participatory evaluation of information systems to enable business benefits to be realised. It is recognised here that easy to use instruments are an essential part of a method for evaluating information systems effectively and that a method cannot be operationalised without them. ABR proposes some instruments focused on benefit realisation, which may complement other modelling, project management, analysis and design instruments currently used in an organisation

9. SUMMARY AND CONCLUSION

In information systems evaluation what must be evaluated are the outcomes of implementing the information system. In other words how the information system supports the organisation and its staff to meet the business goals set by management in the context of the overall organisational strategy.

The formative evaluation process in information systems development may be characterised as a continuous participative process involving a learning process from the participants influencing the design and as part of the learning process a redirecting process from the leadership to ensure that the design meets the current needs.

The ABR approach explicitly integrates and gives importance to evaluation as a way of focusing on and realising business value. The approach is characterised as: systematic, problem oriented, participative, based on a formative evaluation process incorporating milestone evaluations to mark progress in systems development. It is recognised that evaluation instruments are required to support an effective evaluation process.

5

Outcomes and Benefit Modelling for Information Systems Investment

'The ideas of economists and political philosophers, both when they are right and when they are wrong, are more powerful than is commonly understood. Indeed the world is ruled by little else. Practical men, who believe themselves to be quite exempt from any intellectual influence, are usually the slaves of some defunct economist.'

John Maynard Keynes, The General Theory of Employment, Interest and Money, 1936.

1. INTRODUCTION

In this chapter the importance of modelling in the planning and management of an information system is discussed. Three different levels of modelling are specifically addressed which are referred to as *macro*, *meso*[1] and *micro* models.

---

[1] The word meso has been borrowed from the Greek word *meso* meaning middle or in between and has been used in exactly the same way. Thus a meso-model encompasses a level of detail in between the macro model and the micro model.

The understanding of the outcome[2] of an information system and the benefits[3] associated therewith is an essential element in the successful planning and management of any information system implementation (Remenyi and Sherwood-Smith 1996a). When used correctly a benefit model can deliver a rich picture of the benefit potential and the cost implications of a proposed information system. In addition, by changing the assumptions used in developing the model, the information systems planner or sponsor may obtain a greater insight into the issues which are most critical to the success of the implementation. Models are primarily used for their explanatory power and to help understand the impact of changes in the assumptions which underpin the suggested project.

In most organisations the information system sponsor requires a detailed understanding of how the outcome may be achieved and how the benefit stream produced as a result of an investment may be generated, as well as to be able to appreciate the costs of implementing the system. One of the most effective tools available to assist with this is business or financial modelling. Furthermore, the sponsor of an information systems project should be in a position to present the purpose of the project, and especially the benefits which will accrue for the organisation as a result of the investment, to the investment authorising group[4]

---

[2] In this context the outcome is the new circumstances created by the information system after it has been successfully commissioned and implemented. It is the outcome of the system when used appropriately by the business which generates benefits.

[3] An information system's benefit is an improvement in performance which may be measured in some way by the organisation. An information system's benefit does not, per se, have a direct financially measurable implication for the organisation, but might rather be an improvement in quality of customer service etc.

[4] In some organisations this group may be top managers, while in others it may be the eventual users themselves. The more involvement from the eventual users the greater the likelihood of success.

in a convincing way. To achieve this it is helpful to produce a business model of the benefits so they are clearly understood by all the stakeholders.

There is a long tradition in business that capital expenditure needs to be formally justified in terms of the benefits which it will help accrue to the organisation. Thus when a new machine is to be acquired, or when a fleet of vehicles are to be purchased, or when a new factory is to be built, a capital investment appraisal is sometimes, if not frequently, undertaken. Capital investment appraisal usually involves a statement of the initial investment cost, the on-going costs, and the anticipated benefits, as well as the calculation of a number of suitable[5] investment performance indicators or statistics.

It is frequently difficult to formally justify investments in information systems (Ward *et al.* 1996; Lester and Willcocks 1994). This is because reliable estimates of information systems costs and benefits are not always available or easy to obtain. This is, at least in part, due to the complex nature of the impact of information systems on organisations which frequently leads to a portfolio of tangible and intangible benefits.

2. WHAT ARE MODELS?

In general a model may be described as a representation of an artefact, a construction, a system or an event or sequence of events. The representation may be abstracted into symbols, equations and numbers, i.e. mathematical expectations; it may consist of a picture or a drawing, or a fabricated likeness such as

---

[5] There are many different investment performance indicators or statistics which include the return on investment, payback, net present value, internal rate of return and profitability index to mention only a few.

a model aeroplane, or it may be an expression of a situation or relationship in words. A complex model may contain several of these representations simultaneously. The purposes of modelling are many and various, and include developing a fuller understanding of the relationship between the inputs, the process and the outputs of the issue being studied, as well as calculating the likely results of a project. Models are produced to facilitate decision making in the management process (Akkermans 1995; Proctor 1995) and to help in this respect with what-if questions and the extent to which this is achieved is often regarded as a measure of a model's success (Karlin 1983). On the other hand models are sometimes produced for the purposes of simply seeing how a result may appear[6].

There are distinctly different levels of modelling. High level or macro models employ general concepts, or rough drawings, or imprecise fabrications. The purpose of the macro model is to present a conceptual picture which will contextualise the problem or opportunity as well as provide a suggested solution. An intermediate or meso level model will add some detail, perhaps to the form or the structure and may also express the dimensions of the problem and proposed solution, but will still be expressed primarily in generalities. A detailed or micro level model attempts to be closer to reality and thus to use more specific or life-like representations or values. The primary purpose of the micro model is to understand the impact of the proposed solution or course of action. However, all models are by their nature simplifications of the reality which they represent (Zelm *et al.* 1995). In fact sometimes the simpler the model the more meaningfully it may be used (Koella 1991; Maynard Smith

---

[6] Of course models, mostly physical ones fabricated in plastic or wood, are also produced for purely entertainment purposes such as those found in toy and hobby shops which are produced specifically for children and hobbyists.

1975). This is in keeping with the concept of Occam's razor[7] (American Heritage Dictionary 1992). Complex models may actually cloud the central nature of the issues being studied and thus reduce the explanatory power and consequently the value of the model. Examples of the three levels of model, i.e. the macro, the meso and the micro will be discussed later in the chapter.

3. INFORMATION SYSTEM MODELLING

There are various forms of information system modelling. A systems specification is a model. Information systems also use data models and process models. A statement or a drawing of the organisation chart or structure in which the information systems will operate may be seen as an information model. A statement of the hardware configuration of a personal computer may be regarded as a model of the system. The information systems department's budget for expenditure is also a model.

4. OUTCOME OR BENEFIT MODELLING

It is important to distinguish between the concepts of information systems outcome and information systems benefit. The outcome of an information systems investment is the potential[8] which that information system offers to facilitate the

---

[7] In general terms Occam's razor suggests that the simplest solution to a problem is often the best solution. According to the Concise Columbia Encyclopedia 'William of Occam is remembered for his use of the principle of parsimony, formulated as "Occam's razor," which enjoined economy in explanation with the axiom "It is vain to do with more what can be done with less." '

[8] As the information system itself does not per se deliver benefits, but rather benefits are produced when the information system is used to facilitate improvements in business processes, it is therefore possible to see the outcome of an information system as only a potential which will need to be exploited by business users.

delivery of improved business performance, whereas an information systems benefit is the improvement in performance which is achieved by the utilisation of that facility. An important issue which underlies this discussion is the proposition that information systems do not in themselves directly produce benefits. Information systems facilitate business improvements which can increase organisational performance (Ward 1996). This increase in organisational performance is contingent upon the information systems outcome. The outcome represents the whole or the part of the mechanism by which the benefits of the information system, and the change in procedures which it involves, are put in place in order that the benefits will be delivered. Thus the outcome of an information system is the production of changes, or improvements in procedures, which directly lead to business benefits. Information systems outcomes are an intrinsic part of the business model which may help with this process of benefit realisation. The first issue to discuss is the level of the detail of the model.

5. DIFFERENT LEVELS OF MODEL

As mentioned above there are three distinct levels of modelling which correspond to differences in detail and corresponding quantification. These will each be discussed in turn.

5.1 Macro or high level models

High level models express the situation which they represent in general terms. In the context of information systems outcome and benefit modelling this could be the statement of the problem or opportunity which the information system will address. The important issue with a macro model is a high level of conceptual clarity so that all the stakeholders involved understand exactly what is being proposed, how it is envisaged that it will work, and what the expected outcomes and benefits are. An example of a high level outcome and benefit model could be the following:

> Average gross sales invoice values are generally too small to provide the required return on investment. If the average gross sales invoice value is increased by a factor of five, then the cost of administration will come into line with the industry average and this will result in a higher profit and thus a satisfactory return on investment. The average gross sales invoice values may be increased by more effective selection of clients as well as by a greater concentration on cross selling. Clients may be more effectively selected if the relevant sales persons have access to appropriate sales history and market potential information. Similarly, appropriate information systems may enhance the opportunity for cross selling by identifying potential needs for a wider range of our products in our already established client base.

The above statement qualifies as a model because:

1. it is a clear description of a problem, a proposed process which is expected to improve the situation, and it suggests a likely result;

2. it facilitates a discussion of the proposed intervention and possible alternative courses of action.

It is frequently useful to present a macro model in diagrammatic form such as that shown in Figure 5.1 below.

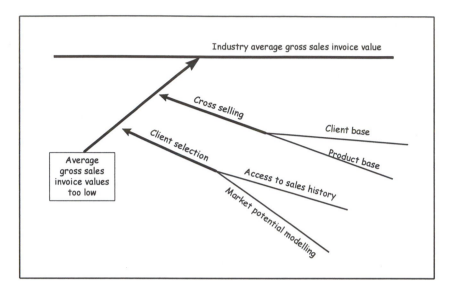

Figure 5.1: A macro model shown in diagrammatic form

This type of macro model, which does not require much time or effort to develop, may be used as a filter which will prevent unsuitable ideas, or ideas which have not yet been developed with sufficient conceptual clarity to be understandable, from being pursued and thus attract scarce resources. Without a macro model in place it is unlikely that a suitable or useful meso or micro model will be produced.

5.2 Meso or intermediate level models

An intermediate level model expands on the high level concepts by adding considerably more detail, especially in the area of the results of the proposed idea. The above example relating to the average gross sales invoice values would be expanded by specifying the particular issues which the system would have to address if the desired outcomes and associated benefits were to be achieved. These variables will be stated in terms of the effectiveness of the system. Thus a sales administration and potential prospect identification system could have business outcomes which deliver the ability to:

---

1. Identify the high value and low value customers;

2. Establish a minimum effective sales order value by product;

3. Establish likely complementary goods for special offers to customers in order to increase sales invoice value;

4. Forecast clients' requirements through the use of purchasers' historical records;

5. Facilitate cross selling of complementary products and services.

The above outcomes will result in the following specific benefits:

1. Higher average invoice value,

2. Lower administrative costs,

3. Better customer service,

4. Better utilisation of inventory,

5. Better utilisation of transport,

6. Better job satisfaction for personnel in sales administration.

A meso model may also include elements of cost. However, in the example which follows the cost dimension has been omitted in order to focus on the more difficult aspect of the business outcomes and the benefits.

For business outcomes and the corresponding benefits related thereto, to be achieved they need to be measurable[9], i.e. a stakeholder should be able to assess whether they have been delivered. Thus it is necessary to establish metrics which may be associated with any outcomes or benefits that have been specified as stemming from the information system's investment. The establishment of a metric will allow a more objective[10] assessment to be made of the extent to which the information system has delivered the business outcomes or benefits.

As stated above, each identified benefit needs to be assigned a specific metric so as to ascertain whether or not the benefit has been realised. If a suitable metric cannot be identified then the suggested benefit should not be included in the model. Figure 5.2 provides an example of a meso model in which specific benefits and metrics with reference to a sales administration and potential prospect identification system have been specified. It is worthwhile to note that with respect to the majority of the metrics presented in the following table, both ex-ante and ex-post[11] measurements are needed. However, it is usual that no calculation takes place within the meso model. This is essential for comparison purposes.

---

[9] The concept of measurability in this context does not specifically refer to the creation of financial estimates. Thus measures of customer satisfaction or user acceptance which are based on opinion surveys are perfectly suitable.

[10] It is clearly understood by the authors that complete objectivity is an ideal which is unlikely to ever be fully achieved. Thus the aim here is to move away from a situation which is primarily subjective towards a higher level of objectivity.

[11] The term ex-ante is used to describe estimates of the benefits and for that matter also the costs in advance of the investment. Ex-post is used to describe the actual cost and estimates of the achieved benefits after the implementation of the project.

The meso model will often take the form of a flowchart or table as shown above but not usually a diagram which is more appropriate for the macro model.

Figure 5.2 qualifies as a model because it describes the outcomes of the information systems and how these outcomes may be used to generate benefits as well as stating an appropriate measurement technique and a required metric. Of course these outcomes or business benefits may be tangible or intangible. At this stage no attempt has been made to quantify the outcome of the proposed benefits which is left for the next level of model.

5.3 The detailed or micro model

The detailed or micro model takes the issues described in the meso model and attempts to quantify them. This quantification may be undertaken in terms of financial estimates, or it may be performed quite differently such as using estimates of customer satisfaction and user acceptability of the proposed system[12]. The low or micro model described in Figure 5.3 attempts to associate financial values with the proposed investment. Note that estimates of costs have been included here in order to allow the return on investment (ROI), which is a popular investment performance indicator, to be calculated.

---

[12] The quantification of benefits can be quite difficult. The primary benefits of some systems will essentially be simple functional requirements which will either exist or not exist. Such benefits will be evaluated on a yes/no binary scale and no further quantification is really possible without stretching assumptions beyond an acceptable level. Others will be more relative in nature and those benefits that can be evaluated on a qualitative scale [very good, good, satisfactory, poor, very poor] which may be converted to a measurable agreed numeric scale. Other benefits, for example, 'Average Invoice Value' can be measured on a £ per Invoice scale and a target set to define a satisfactory business result from the information system development project.

Business Outcome	Specific Benefits	Measurement Method	Specific Metric
Better return on the firm's sales efforts	**Better customer service**	Customer satisfaction surveys	
		1) Distributed questionnaires	SERVQUAL Determination of expected service and the service which the customer perceives.
		2) Personal interviews	Qualitative data to be analysed using interpretative techniques.
Forecast clients' requirements	**Better utilisation of inventory**	Inventory and sales statistics	Inventory turnover. Number of days sales in inventory.
Improve utilisation of corporate assets	**Better employment of transport fleet**	Vehicle tracking system	Petrol consumption.
		Matching vehicles to customer orders	Number of deliveries per day. Number of vehicles on the road vs. number of deliveries.

Business Outcome	Specific Benefits	Measurement Method	Specific Metric
Better utilisation of corporate resources	**Better job satisfaction of personnel from sales administration**	Staff satisfaction survey	Gap between expectations and performance.
Lower cost profile	**Lower administrative costs**	Accounting system	Cost per invoice/credit note etc.

Figure 5.2: A meso model Specific metrics matched to their benefits for a sales administration and potential prospect identification system

A low level or micro model		
Initial investment costs		1350
Hardware	500	
Software	450	
Data communications	150	
Commissioning	250	
On-going costs		130
Staff	50	
Maintenance	45	
Accomodation	25	
General expenses	10	
Benefits		275
Reduction in administrative costs	20	
Better utilisation of inventory	75	
Better utilisation of transport	30	
Additional income arising from sales improvement	150	
Net benefit		145
Annualised benefit		1740
ROI		129%

Figure 5.3: The low or micro model showing cost benefit analysis

The type of statement shown in Figure 5.3 is readily identifiable as a financial model usually produced by accountants. It is by far the most frequently used type of model in capital investment appraisal.

In a detailed or micro model it is not necessary for the estimates of the variables to be accurate. In fact it is always understood that they will not be so. This model is only required to indicate the general direction of what the results of the project may look like. As shown in Figure 5.3 this model is described as a deterministic evaluation of the situation and for a richer understanding of the situation it will need to be developed into a stochastic evaluation. This will be discussed in the Chapter Six.

6. THE ISSUE OF TANGIBLE AND INTANGIBLE BENEFITS

In developing an outcome or benefit model it is important to incorporate both tangible and intangible benefits, especially at the macro and meso levels and this has already been demonstrated above. Some intangible benefits are receptive to modelling at the micro level and thus where possible this should also be undertaken.

For example, it is possible to list the advantages and disadvantages of a particular course of action and then balance the conflicting interests which these issues represent. Another example of a low level model of intangible benefits is that of planning a particular profile of user information systems satisfaction and an appropriate pictorial model is shown in Figure 5.4.

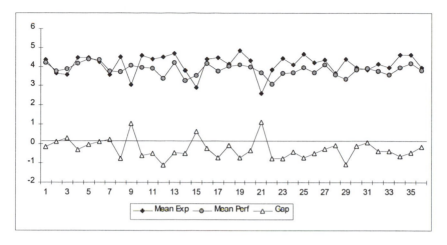

Figure 5.4: A user satisfaction model

This type of model has a number of uses including the allocation of resources to different aspects of an information systems infrastructure, especially with regards to establishing the service level requirements. The organisation may plan different levels of satisfaction for different aspects of the information systems service by managing either the expectation levels or alternatively managing the resources available to deliver the appropriate amount of support and thus the eventual satisfaction level.

A tangible information system benefit is one which directly affects the firm's profitability, whereas an intangible information system benefit is one which can be seen to have a positive effect on the firm's business, but does not necessarily directly influence the firm's profitability (Remenyi *et al.* 1995). Thus with an intangible benefit the cause and effect relationship may not be clearly visible and thus fully understood.

Within the broad categories of tangible and intangible benefits a further classification is required as different types of benefit may be quantifiable or unquantifiable or easily measurable or difficult to measure.

A quantifiable tangible information system benefit is one which directly affects the firm's profitability, and the effect of which is such that it may be objectively measured. For example, reduction in costs or assets or an increase in revenue. An unquantifiable tangible information system benefit can also be seen to directly affect the firm's profitability, but the precise extent to which it does cannot be directly measured. Examples include the ability to obtain better information through the use of an information system, improving the corporate risk profile and improving the firm's security.

Intangible benefits can also be sub-classified in the same way. A quantifiable intangible information system benefit is one which can be measured, but its impact does not necessarily directly affect the firm's profitability. For example, obtaining information faster, providing better customer satisfaction or improved staff satisfaction. Perhaps the most difficult type of information system benefit is the unquantifiable[13] intangible benefit. This refers to benefits that cannot easily be measured and the impact of the benefit does not necessarily directly affect the firm's profitability. Examples include improved market reaction to the firm, customer perception or potential future employees' perception of the firm's product.

These different types of generic information system benefits can be illustrated in a two by two matrix as shown in Figure 5.5.

---

[13] It is sometimes suggested that the unquantifiable intangible benefits are so distant from delivering real value that they should not be included in any business analysis. The authors have included them here primarily for the sake of completeness.

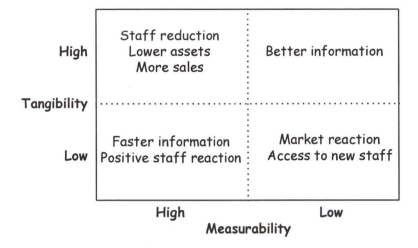

Figure 5.5: Information system output/benefit matrix

The different benefit types described above can be measured using specific modelling techniques. These may be seen in Figure 5.6.

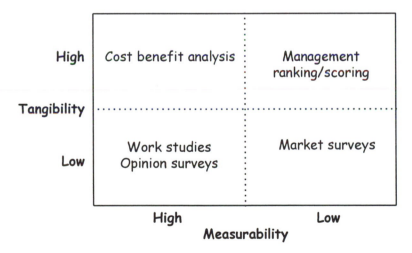

Figure 5.6: Benefit measurement techniques

There are several different types of cost benefit analysis which may be used to measure the effect of staff reductions, lower assets or more sales in financial terms. The techniques for modelling these situations are discussed in the Chapter Six. Internal opinion surveys and their analysis are also reviewed, while general market survey techniques are addressed. Management ranking and scoring techniques are reviewed. It is generally believed that cost benefit analysis is the *hard* measure while the other measures are *soft*.

7. TANGIBLE AND INTANGIBLE COSTS

In the same way as there are tangible and intangible benefits there may also be said to be tangible and intangible costs. It is also possible to make the distinction between costs which are relatively easy to measure and those which are problematical.

The definition of a tangible cost is that it will directly affect the profit in an adverse way while an intangible cost, which may also be referred to as a dis-benefit (Remenyi *et al.* 1995), may be defined as one which will cause problems[14] which will indirectly lead to an increased cost profile.

Figure 5.7 shows how different types of costs may be categorised using the tangible and the measurability dimensions.

---

[14] There are of course a whole range of costs which are normally not quantified, such as the cost of setting up a project team. Sometimes these may be regarded as intangible costs while at other times these are seen as tangible costs which are not itemised as they are more properly included in the overhead structure of the organisation.

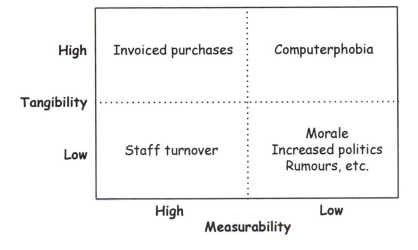

Figure 5.7: Information system cost matrix

The issue of staff turnover is placed in a quadrant which is low on tangibility as it may be argued that the real cost of losing staff is not so much the expense of recruitment of a new member of staff but rather the disruption costs which occur due to the induction period required by a new person before they become fully productive.

8. SUMMARY AND CONCLUSION

Outcomes and benefit modelling is of critical importance for information systems investment planning. It is most important that all three levels of modelling are undertaken in order that management will have a comprehensive understanding of how the proposed information systems is likely to impact the organisation, and thus see how it may be used to drive improvements in performance and create a positive benefit stream.

If outcome and benefit models are not adequately produced there is little likelihood that the central issues on which improved business performance and its resulting benefit flows will be understood. This is simply because the modelling process is one of the most effective ways by which executives can appreciate the impact information systems have on their organisations. Without this insight it is virtually impossible to achieve this level of understanding.

6

Micro Modelling Information Systems Outcomes and Benefits

'We are merely reminding ourselves that human decision affecting the future, whether personal or political or economic, cannot depend on strict mathematical expectations, since the basis for making such calculations does not exist; and that it is our innate urge to activity which makes the wheels go round, our rational selves choosing between the alternatives as best we are able, calculating where we can, but often falling back for our motive or whim or sentiment or chance'

John Maynard Keynes, The General Theory of Employment, Interest and Money, 1936.

1. INTRODUCTION

Chapter Five contained a high level discussion of the nature of modelling and the role it plays in information systems development. This chapter discusses the detail of producing cost benefit models which describe the introduction of information systems to an organisation.

There are many different categories of both costs and benefits which are relevant to information systems development environments and it is essential that all the appropriate elements are generally addressed in the analysis of the investment. Unlike

IS benefits, the concept of IS costs is relatively well understood and therefore does not need any further elaboration or definition. However, in connection with IS the term *hidden cost* is sometimes encountered. A hidden cost is a non-obvious cost of IS which may in fact appear in another department or function as a result of computerisation. According to Willcocks (1991) operations and maintenance costs are sometimes considered to be hidden and these may amount to as much as two to ten times the development and installation costs over the first four years of the life of an IS project. As the impact of IS has become more and more understood there is less and less scope for costs to be hidden.

The term *opportunity cost* is also sometimes used. The opportunity cost of an investment or project is the amount which the firm could earn if the sum invested was used in another way. Thus the opportunity cost of a computer system might be the amount which would be earned if the funds were invested in the core business, or if the funds were placed in an appropriate bank account.

It is interesting to note that the costs of implementing new IS systems have changed dramatically over the past 20 years. According to Bjørn-Andersen (1986) the organisational costs have increased from about 20% to 50%. Of course this trend is bound to continue for quite some time. This is clearly shown in Figure 6.1.

It is sometimes argued that when producing a micro model the cost estimates of a system should be based on the ownership costs over a projected five year system life. Systems lasting longer than this period will produce a bonus for the organisation. Systems which do not remain in place for five years may produce negative results, but this does not necessarily mean that the investment should not be undertaken.

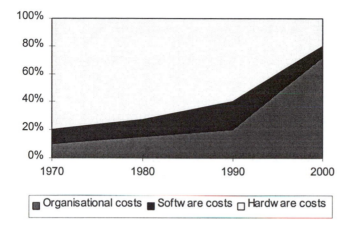

Figure 6.1: Increase in organisational costs incurred during IS implementation

2. THE COST BENEFIT MODEL

The cost benefit model is by far the most popular model which is undertaken in order to determine whether an information systems investment should take place. There are a considerable number of different approaches to these and the following sections discuss some of the more important variations of cost benefit modelling.

2.1 The nature of cost benefit analysis

Cost benefit analysis may be defined as the process of comparing the various financial costs of acquiring and implementing an information system with the tangible and measurable benefits which the organisation derives from the use of the system. Thus, referring to Figures 5.5 and 5.7 in Chapter Five, by definition cost benefit analysis only concerns itself with the top left quadrant. This means that a cost benefit analysis of any information systems project can only deliver the financial dimension of the equation. This cost benefit model needs to be supported by models describing the less financially tangible and measurable aspects

In general cost benefit analysis should be performed on a marginal costing basis. This means that only additional costs incurred by the new system should be included. Likewise only marginal benefits, i.e. new or additional benefits, should be compared to the costs.

It is often thought that only benefits are difficult to estimate. However, as many if not most IS projects over-run in terms of their cost, this is clearly not so. Considerable care should be given to cost estimation, especially where software development is concerned. Also on-going costs are regularly undetected and therefore these should be carefully scrutinised.

Different approaches to cost benefit analysis are required for automate, informate and transformate investments (Zuboff 1988). An automate investment attempts to improve the organisation's efficiency by the use of computers to automate tasks which were previously undertaken on a manual basis. An informate investment is one which attempts to deliver information in such a way that management may make better decisions and thus direct the organisation so that its objectives are more effectively achieved. A transformate investment changes the way the organisation conducts its business so that new and better process or products or markets are exploited. The following are among the most important approaches to cost benefit modelling which address these different types of investment.

2.2 The cost displacement model

Cost displacement considers the cost of the investment and compares this to the other costs which the system has saved. This is typically used in the more traditional data processing environments where computers are used to replace clerical workers or even sometimes blue collar workers. These are often referred to as automate systems as described in the previous paragraph. It is not really appropriate for situations where the IS system will add value rather than reduce costs. A cost displacement justification is a classical automate situation, although it may also have informate implications. Figure 6.2 shows an example of cost displacement analysis for one year. It should be noted that the costs and benefits are marginal.

The cost displacement approach shown in Figure 6.2 to assessing an IS investment proposition is an *ex-ante* analysis of what the firm plans to achieve. It is nothing more than a statement of intent. To ensure that these intentions are carried out, a list of details about the system and the environment in which it will function should also be supplied. An outline action detail list is supplied in Figure 6.3 for the above cost displacement proposal. For complex information systems this list could be a dozen pages long.

It is sometimes preferable to perform this type of cost benefit modelling over a number of years. There is much to be said about the pros and cons of three years and five years. However such detail is beyond the scope of this book.

Cost Displacement Model - 1 year		
Investment cost		1,305,000
Hardware	545,000	
Software	350,000	
Communications	125,000	
Infrastructure	75,000	
Staff related costs	125,000	
Commissioning	85,000	
On-going costs		125,000
Staff	55,000	
Accommodation	45,000	
Training and development	15,000	
General expenses	10,000	
Benefits		162,500
Staff savings	60,000	
Accommodation	95,000	
Reduction in asset requirements	7,500	
Net benefit per month		37,500
Net annualised benefit		450,000
ROI		0.34
Payback		2.9 years

Figure 6.2[1]: The cost displacement approach 1 year

There is considerable debate as to whether IS investments should be planned on a three, five or even seven year horizon. Some firms use a three year period for personal computers, a five year period for mid-range systems and a six or seven year period for mainframes. However, a growing number of practitioners believe that three to five years is the maximum period for which IS should be planned. This relatively short period, however, does produce problems for some large scale

---

[1] As Figure 6.2 shows only a one year period no discounted cash flow measures have been calculated.

systems which may take three years to develop. Obviously in such cases a longer time horizon should be used[2].

1.	List of the jobs which will be affected by the new system. Against each job a date by which the change will occur should be stated.
2.	List of individuals, by name, whose work will change.
3.	List of supervisors and managers, by name, who will be affected.
4.	An indication, by name, of the staff which will no longer be required in their functions after the system is fully operating.
5.	Plans for staff transfer or staff redundancy.
6.	List the office space which will be released by the reduction in staff.
7.	Indicate which other departments require the released space.
8.	Indicate how the space can be re-let to other enterprises.
9.	Indicate which leases are coming up for review and may therefore be terminated.
10.	A timetable for the occurrence of each of the above.

Responsibility for the above Mr J.J. Jones

Figure 6.3: The action detail for a cost displacement approach

2.3 The cost avoidance model

A cost avoidance analysis is similar to cost displacement but in this case no cost has been removed from the system because the introduction of IS has prevented cost from being incurred. This type of system is also typically used in the more traditional data

---

[2] There are several other issues related to the horizon of the investment which relate to economic life expectancy, terminal value and to taxation legislation. However these issues are beyond the scope of this book.

processing environments and is generally less relevant to more modern IS applications. Thus, like cost displacement, cost avoidance is most appropriate in automate systems. Figure 6.4 shows an example of cost avoidance analysis.

Cost Avoidance Model - 1 year		
Investment cost		**1,650,000**
Hardware	455,000	
Software	760,000	
Communications	250,000	
Infrastructure	85,000	
Staff related costs	65,000	
Commissioning	35,000	
On-going costs		**135,000**
Staff	75,000	
Accommodation	30,000	
Training and development	25,000	
General expenses	5,000	
Benefits		**169,000**
Staff savings	55,000	
Accommodation	105,000	
Reduction in asset requirements	9,000	
Net benefit per month		**34,000**
Net annualised benefit		**408,000**
ROI		25%
Payback		4 years

Figure 6.4: The cost avoidance approach

2.4 The decision analysis model

Decision analysis attempts to evaluate the benefits to be derived from the availability of better information which is assumed to lead to better decisions. In turn, it is believed that better decisions lead to better performance. As it is hard to define good information, let alone good decisions, cost benefit analysis using this method is generally considered to be difficult.

Decision analysis is a classic informate situation which requires a financial value to be associated with the improvements which will result from information being available to managers. In some cases, it is relatively easy to measure the effect of the availability information, although there will frequently be considerable noise in the environment which may obscure some of the effects of the system. The key to decision analysis is to perform rigorous business analysis of the situation before the introduction of the proposed technology. The types of business relationships at work and their effects on each other should be understood. Also how the proposed information system will improve these business relationships, should be explained. A model of how information is used in the firm to make decisions and how these decisions impact upon actions which in turn affect performance is useful when conducting decision analysis. Such a model is shown in Figure 6.5.

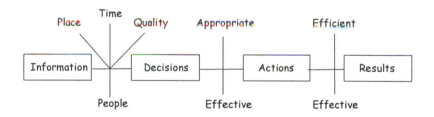

Figure 6.5: Decision analysis model indicating the relationship between information[3] and results

---

[3] Sometimes this model begins with data which if processed in an appropriate manner becomes information. It has been decided that this aspect of the model has become well accepted and fairly routine for many organisations and thus the key elements actually only come into play after the information has been produced.

The model in Figure 6.5 suggests how information of a higher quality, delivered to the right people, at the right time, may be used to make better decisions. Better decisions implemented effectively and efficiently will lead to better action. Better action which is appropriately directed, monitored and controlled will lead to better performance which will translate to more profit and cash.

Figure 6.6 is an example of a micro model for decision analysis. This case relies on understanding how the firm's credit control works, how the cash flow functions, and how investment availability impacts sales. In fact each line under the heading of benefits would be derived by reference to the logic described in Figure 6.5.

Decision Analysis Model - 1 year		
Investment cost		**1,650,000**
Hardware	455,000	
Software	760,000	
Communications	250,000	
Infrastructure	85,000	
Staff related costs	65,000	
Commissioning	35,000	
On-going costs		**135,000**
Staff	75,000	
Accommodation	30,000	
Training and development	25,000	
General expenses	5,000	
Benefits		**175,000**
Reduction in bad debts	25,000	
Interest earned by faster receipts	10,000	
Reduction in obsolete inventories	20,000	
Increased sales due to better availability	120,000	
Net benefit per month		**40,000**
Net annualised benefit		**480,000**
ROI		29%
Payback		3 years

Figure 6.6: The decision analysis approach

For example, the benefit item reduction in bad debts is calculated with reference to how the proposed information systems will supply quality information at the right time and at the right place to the credit control staff. The credit controller then states how the staff will be able to use this information to make better decisions and what sort of action these decisions will give rise to. Finally the credit control staff will estimate the financial consequences of their being able to take better focused actions as a result of these decisions. This process is repeated with the corporate treasurer for the second line item in the benefit section of Figure 6.6, with the logistics manager for the third line item and the sales manager for the fourth line item.

Thus the information-decision-action-result model described in Figure 6.5 actually drives the calculation of the numbers in the cost benefit analysis shown in Figure 6.6.

2.5 The business impact or time release analysis model

Business impact analysis or time release analysis attempts to quantify the effect that IS can have on the physical performance of employees while undertaking a particular course of work. This time release analysis may have elements of automate, informate and even transformate, depending on the exact circumstances involved.

The primary benefit of time release is that staff may do other work, and when this involves acquiring extra sales it may contribute to transforming the business. Figure 6.7 shows an example of impact analysis.

```
Impact Analysis Model - 1 year

Investment cost                                          70,000
Hardware                                      30,000
Software                                      25,000
Communications                                 5,000
Infrastructure                                 2,000
Staff related costs                            5,000
Commissioning                                  3,000

On-going costs                                           14,000
Staff                                         10,000
Accommodation                                  1,000
Training and development                       2,000
General expenses                               1,000

Benefits - total time release                        170 minutes
Average length of sales call before            35 minutes
Average number of sales calls per day              6
Average value of sales per call                2,500
Reduction in average sales call time           20 minutes
Reduction in time required for daily form filling  50 minutes

Average travel time between sales calls        25 minutes
Additional number of sales calls possible          2
Additional revenue generated per day           5,000
Additional revenue generated per month       110,000
Net profit %                                     15%
Additional profit per month                   16,500

Net benefit per month                                    2,500
Net annualised benefit                                  30,000

ROI                                                       43%
Payback                                               2 years
```

Figure 6.7: The impact or time release model

The impact, or time release model in Figure 6.9 is a micro model which describes the introduction of hand held computers to a number of sales people. As a result of this new technology the sales people are able to make sales calls on small supermarkets in 15 minutes rather than taking the original 35 minutes. In addition, as the day's work is logged in the hand held computer as it happens the sales people are saved some of the day-end paperwork which they traditionally completed.

The result of this system is that the sales people equipped with the hand held computers have extra time which they use to make more sales calls and in so doing they are able to generate more sales. The increase in profit from these marginal sales earns a return on the investment in the hand held computers of 43% and thus earns a payback for the system in two years.

2.6 How to estimate the possible financial value of an intangible benefit

As mentioned earlier intangible benefits may also be modelled. In this respect benefits such as user satisfaction may be directly included in a macro and a meso model. In a micro model, user satisfaction would have to be estimated using a Servqual[4] scale. However some organisations would not regard this as sufficient and they would attempt to place a money value on such an intangible benefit.

A typical intangible IS benefit is the ability of management to perform what-if analysis on financial plans and budgets. More information of this type is clearly advantageous and valuable to management, but it is difficult to associate a particular financial amount with this type of benefit.

There are two main ways of evaluating intangible benefits[5]. The first approach is by negotiation and the second approach is by imputation.

---

[4] Servqual is a scale created by Parasuraman *et al.* (1988), which is a recognised measure of user satisfaction with a service. This theory, which was initially developed for marketing, has been adopted and adapted for use with information systems management.

[5] It is sometimes argued that there are only two ways of estimating the financial value of intangible benefits and that all other ways are derived from these two methods.

The following describes two situations in which these techniques have been attempted.

2.6.1 Negotiating intangible benefits

The first step in evaluating this type of benefit is to ask the managers who are using this facility to place a value on it. This may be done by asking a series of questions such as: Would you pay £10 for this report? If the answer is yes, then the next question would be: Would you pay £10,000 for this report? If the answer is no, then an iterative binary division may be conducted to find the value of the facility to the user. An iterative binary division search refers to a computer algorithm which in this context would involve adding the first suggested amount, i.e. £10 to the second suggested amount, i.e. £10,000 and then dividing the sum by two. The resulting number of £5005 would then be suggested to the manager as the value of the intangible benefit. If this number is rejected then the £5005 will be added to the £10 and again divided by two. This would result in an offer of £2507.50. If this is rejected the process continues until an amount is accepted. The value so derived may be considered as the size of the intangible benefit. Of course, this approach produces a subjective evaluation of the benefit. However, it does result in a number as opposed to a simple comfort statement, and the number may be used in a cost benefit analysis calculation to see if the investment makes sense. This approach may be considered to be semi-hard or semi-soft analysis and is sometimes referred to as benefit negotiation.

2.6.2 Imputing intangible benefits

An imputed benefit value is one which is derived by calculating the amount an information system must be worth to the firm if it is to proceed with the investment and earn its required rate of return. The required rate of return which is also known as the cost of capital is the percentage return which an investment needs to earn if the economic or financial value of the organisation is not to be reduced by the investment. This of course assumes that the firm remains economically rational and that the cost of capital is known.

An example of imputing an intangible benefit could be as illustrated in Figure 6.8:

1.	A system is required in order to enhance the working conditions in an office.
2.	There are no immediately obvious tangible benefits.
3.	The cost of the system is £300,000.
4.	The cost of capital to the firm is 25%.

Figure 6.8: Imputing an intangible benefit

This means that the firm can earn £75,000 (£300,000 multiplied by 25%) by investing this amount in debtors, inventory, machines and equipment etc.

It can therefore be argued that in order to justify this investment the firm needs to be able to show a benefit of £75,000 because if this is not the case the investment in the information systems will actually be devaluing the organisation.

2.7 The transformate model

The type of analysis or modelling which is used to assess a transformate opportunity is the same as that analysis employed for any strategic investment. Strategic investments often involve many considerations which are particularly difficult to quantify. Issues such as competitive advantage, market share, new product development are just a few examples. Strategic investments are frequently considered so important that a full *ex-ante* cost justification may not be undertaken[6], or if it is, the results of the analysis may simply be ignored. Statements such as 'it's too important to ignore' or 'the cost of not doing it will be crippling' are frequently heard in association with strategic investments. Therefore, strategic investment appraisal studies will often contain more words than numbers. The descriptive part of the proposal will contain words such as, *'This opportunity is so important that it is impossible for us to ignore.'* In effect this means that more emphasis is being placed on the macro model than on either the meso or the micro model and this practice illustrates that for certain types of investment it may not be necessary to undertake the lower level modelling.

Good practice, however, requires meso and micro modelling and thus some numeric analysis should be performed. As transformate or strategic investments will usually have a longer time frame implication than efficiency or effectiveness investments, the simple ROI and payback methods are usually not adequate. The time value of money based techniques required for discounted cash flow analysis need to be used.

For micro models using discounted cash flow techniques more data and assumptions are generally required. This technique is shown in Figure 6.9.

---

[6] There is a peculiar logic which is sometimes exercised by top management which is that an investment may be so important that it is not necessary to delay its initiation by submitting it to any of the standard capital investment appraisal procedures.

A micro model for a transformate proposal

Investment cost				**2,895,000**
Staff related costs			1,200,000	
Commissioning			790,000	
Communications			350,000	
Infrastructure			555,000	

On-going costs				**370,000**
Staff			125,000	
Accommodation			75,000	
Training and development			45,000	
General expenses			125,000	

	Year 1	Year 2	Year 3	Year 4
Benefits				
Marginal increase in revenue	2,000,000	2,100,000	2,205,000	2,315,250
Marginal increase in costs	820,000	902,000	992,200	1,091,420
Marginal increase in profit before tax	1,180,000	1,198,000	1,212,800	1,223,830
Tax	354,000	359,400	363,840	367,149
Marginal increase in profit after tax	826,000	838,600	848,960	856,681
Add back depreciation	400,000	400,000	400,000	400,000
Net Cash Flow	**1,226,000**	**1,238,600**	**1,248,960**	**1,256,681**

Firm's cost of capital		20%
Tax rate		30%
Net present value		315,622
Profitability index		1.11

Figure 6.9: A micro model for a transformate proposal

Although it is beyond the scope of this book to discuss the detail of the calculation for discounted cash flow it is necessary to point out that this model requires only marginal cash flow to be exclusively used in the calculation. As depreciation is not a cash expense it is necessary to exclude such costs from the calculations. In addition corporation tax needs to be included as well as an estimation of the cost of capital. Thus the arithmetic work required to produce this micro model is considerably more than the previous example.

In the model for a transformate proposal described in Figure 6.9, an information system allows the organisation to generate additional revenue. This revenue incurs direct and indirect marginal costs. The revenue less the costs produces a before tax marginal profit. Corporation tax is then calculated and subtracted from the pre-tax profit. Because depreciation on the equipment had been included in the costs, it is then necessary to add this amount back. Once this is done the net cash flow figures appear. These numbers are then used to calculate the net present value and the profitability index.

This is a well established approach which is used extensively in many different types of capital investment analysis.

3. DETERMINISTIC vs STOCHASTIC MODELLING

Traditional cost benefit analysis is undertaken using discounted cash flow techniques involving forecasts of the investment amount, the annual or periodic benefits and the cost of capital etc. All these variables are difficult to estimate and the cost of the firm's capital is frequently considered the most difficult variable to determine. The rate of interest which the firm pays on its debt or an arbitrarily chosen hurdle or discount rate is sometimes used as a surrogate for the cost of capital.

As mentioned earlier, IS systems evaluation may be undertaken in several different ways using a variety of measures and at least two different processes. The two processes discussed here are the *deterministic* approach using single point estimates for the input values and generating a single estimate for the result, and the *stochastic* approach which uses ranges as input and generates a range of results. The stochastic method is sometimes referred to as *simulation* or *risk analysis*.

Deterministic analysis[7] assumes a certain world where the exact value of input variables can be known. Once the values of these inputs are entered a unique result, determined by the logic of the algorithm and the precise data, is calculated. Because ex-ante investment analysis exclusively uses estimates of future values for the investment amount, the on-going costs and the benefits, it is frequently said that as soon as the single point values are determined, the input and output will be wrong.

Stochastic analysis[8] which is also known as probability or risk analysis, on the other hand, attempts to accommodate the inherent uncertainty in the world and thus variability in the input estimates and produces a range of possible results which more closely reflects the level of possibilities frequently experienced in the real business world.

In situations where uncertainty is relatively small, deterministic models can provide suitable solutions. However, as is more likely to be the case, uncertainty in the input variables, evidenced by their variability, is likely to be relatively high and therefore this will have to be taken into consideration.

This uncertainty is captured by specifying a probability distribution for each of the input variables such as investment, cash flows, and cost of capital. There are many candidate probability distributions that can be usefully employed for this purpose. Some of the more useful distributions are likely to be the uniform, the triangular and the beta.

---

[7] According to the American Heritage Dictionary of the English Language, Third Edition, deterministic refers to the fact that there is an inevitable consequence of antecedents. Thus once values are specified for the inputs of a deterministic model the result will be unique and easily calculated.

[8] According to the American Heritage Dictionary of the English Language, Third Edition, stochastic refers to involving a random variable or variables and the chance or probability of their occurrence.

Operationalisation of the above is through the use of the Monte Carlo method (Hertz 1968). This involves generating a range of outcomes for the input variables, e.g. investment, described by some specified probability distribution, and then evaluating the behaviour of an associated output variable, for example, the internal rate of return. The Monte Carlo method can also be used to establish how robust and sensitive the outcomes are with respect to the assumptions concerning the input variable(s).

For more on the properties of a number of probability distributions, and guidance on how to generate random samples from these distributions, see Johnson and Kotz (1970) and Gonin and Money (1989). Also within all major spreadsheets there is a facility to create these types of distributions.

3.1 Deterministic modelling

Figure 6.10 shows the data input form of a deterministic model for capital investment appraisal in a spreadsheet, and Figure 6.11 shows the data entered. All the data are single point estimates.

	A	B	C	D	E	F	G	H
1								
2	Capital Investment Appraisal System							
3								
4			Cash-Out	Cash-In	Net Cash Movement each year			
5								
6	IT Investment - Cash Out		?			0		
7	Net IT Benefits	Year 1		?		0		
8		Year 2		?		0		
9		Year 3		?		0		
10		Year 4		?		0		
11		Year 5		?		0		
12								
13	Fixed Cost of Capital or Interest Rate			20.00%				
14				Y1	Y2	Y3	Y4	Y5
15	Inflation Adjusted Interest Rates			?	?	?	?	?
16								
17								
18								

Figure 6.10: The input form for a deterministic model

	A	B	C	D	E	F	G	H
1								
2	Capital Investment Appraisal System							
3								
4			Cash-Out	Cash-In	Net Cash Movement each year			
5								
6	IT Investment - Cash Out		350000		-350000			
7	Net IT Benefits	Year 1		60000	60000			
8		Year 2		95000	95000			
9		Year 3		120000	120000			
10		Year 4		180000	180000			
11		Year 5		200000	200000			
12								
13	Fixed Cost of Capital or Interest Rate			20.00%				
14					Y1	Y2	Y3	Y4	Y5
15	Inflation Adjusted Interest Rates				25.00%	29.00%	30.00%	35.00%	40.00%
16								
17								

Figure 6.11: Completed input form for the deterministic model

The use of discounted cash flow techniques requires that all figures used actually represent cash dispensed or received by the firm. Therefore, profit figures which include non-cash items such as depreciation or reserves should not be used. Figure 6.12 shows the results which use a number of different investment measures including payback, NPV, PI, IRR, etc.

	A	B	C	D	E	F	G	H
21								
22	Investment Reports on IT System							
23								
24	Payback in years & months				3	years	5	months
25	Rate of return(%)				37.43%			
26	N P V Fixed Discount Rate (FDR)				2598			
27	Profitability Index FDR (PI)				1.01			
28	Internal Rate of Return (IRR)				20.28%			
29								
30								
31								
32	Variable Discount Rates							
33	N P V Variable Discount Rates (VDR)				-71754			
34	Profitability Index VDR (PI)				0.79			
35								
36								
37								
38	Discounted Payback FDR in years and months				4	years	11	months

Figure 6.12: Results produced by the deterministic model

An important feature of this model is the use of variable costs for capital or interest rates. These interest rates may be used to reflect either anticipated rates of inflation, or more generally, to adjust for an increasing risk profile. The further into the future the estimated benefit the greater the degree of uncertainty or risk, and therefore the higher the discount or interest rate which is normally associated with the investment. The high interest rate has the effect of reducing the future value of the benefit.

The results shown in Figure 6.12 are, of course, highly dependent upon the assumptions made concerning the cost of capital, the investment amount and the annual cash flows. As these future estimates are always uncertain it is appropriate to perform what-if analysis on these assumptions. Figure 6.13 shows a what-if table indicating the way in which the NPV is related to the cost of capital. Against each cost of capital estimate there is the resulting NPV.

	A	B	C	D
96	Variation in cost of capital and NPV			
97			2598	
98		10%	120342.314	
99		12%	92597.1019	
100		14%	67175.7589	
101		16%	43838.5351	
102		18%	22374.5239	
103		20%	2597.73663	
104		22%	-15656.231	
105		24%	-32533.037	
106		26%	-48162.016	
107		28%	-62658.256	

Figure 6.13: Variation in cost of capital and its impact on the NPV

Figure 6.14 shows the effect of different investment amounts and different costs of capital on the project. As the investment amounts are shown vertically, and the costs of capital are shown horizontally, the resulting NPV may be read from the intersection of the chosen row and column.

	A	B	C	D	E	F	G
110							
111	Variation in cost of capital and investment amount on NPV						
112							
113		2598	200000	250000	300000	350000	400000
114		10%	270342	220342	170342	120342	70342
115		12%	242597	192597	142597	92597	42597
116		14%	217176	167176	117176	67176	17176
117		16%	193839	143839	93839	43839	-6161
118		18%	172375	122375	72375	22375	-27625
119		20%	152598	102598	52598	2598	-47402
120		22%	134344	84344	34344	-15656	-65656
121		24%	117467	67467	17467	-32533	-82533
122		26%	101838	51838	1838	-48162	-98162
123		28%	87342	37342	-12658	-62658	-112658

Figure 6.14: Effect of variation in cost of capital and investment amount on NPV

Thus, with an investment of £70,000 and a cost of capital of 21% the resulting NPV will be £52,880. This sort of multiple what-if analysis is sometimes referred to as sensitivity analysis, although correctly speaking sensitivity analysis is actually a somewhat more complicated matter.

3.2 Stochastic or risk modelling

As mentioned previously, the risk of an investment is the potential of input/output variables to fluctuate from their original estimates. As in the vast majority of cases input/output variables do fluctuate, and risk analysis accommodates this by allowing ranges, rather than single point estimates, to be used. It is generally easier to confidently state that an investment will be between £200,000 and £300,000 than it will be £250,000.

There are a variety of techniques available which assist management in assessing the extent and the size of the risk inherent in a particular investment. There are at least three generic approaches to identifying and assessing risk. These are:

- Group brainstorming

- Expert judgement

- Assumption analysis

Group brainstorming uses group interaction to identify the variables which carry the most exposure to variability. Once the variables have been identified, the group then attempts to quantify the limits of the variability as well as the probability associated with the range of possible inputs and outputs. Brainstorming groups may meet several times before the estimates of the variables are finalised.

Expert judgement uses experienced individuals who are aware of the factors causing the investment potential to vary. This is the quickest and easiest way of identifying risk, but considerable care should be given when choosing the expert.

Assumption analysis requires the detailed questioning of each assumption. This analysis requires each assumption to be modified in such a way that circumstances will be evaluated which are disadvantageous to the investment. The effect of the changes in assumptions are then used as part of the range of variable specification.

Figure 6.15 is a completed input form and Figure 6.16 is the results screens for risk analysis calculations performed for the IRR. Figure 6.17 shows these results graphically.

	A	B	C	D	E	F
1	Input form for Risk Analysis					
2				Minimum	Maximum	
3	IT Investment - Cash Out			350000	400000	
4						
5	Net IT Benefits	Year 1		60000	70000	
6		Year 2		95000	105000	
7		Year 3		120000	130000	
8		Year 4		180000	200000	
9		Year 5		200000	250000	
10						
11	Fixed Cost of Capital			20.00%	30.00%	
12						

Figure 6.15: Completed input form for risk analysis on the IRR

From the data in Figure 6.15 it can be seen that the initial investment amount is not certain, but it is known that it will be between £350,000 and £400,000. Similarly the information systems benefits for years 1 to 5 are also specified as ranges, for example in year 1 the maximum benefit is estimated at £70,000 and the minimum value of the benefit is stated at £60,000. Similarly, the exact rate of interest is not known and it is estimated at between 20% and 30% per annum.

The data used in Figure 6.15 to produce the results in Figures 6.16 and 6.17 would be regarded as being of relatively low risk. The reason for this is that the most likely outcome is a return of 17.5% with a standard deviation of 3.6%. This means that even if all the most unfavourable estimates occur, i.e. maximum investment costs, lowest benefits and highest cost of capital, this investment will still be expected to produce an IRR of 6%. On the positive side, if the investment is kept low and the highest benefits are achieved etc., then this investment could produce a return as high as 28%.

	A	B	C	D	E	F
1						
2						
3				**Summary statistics for**	**IRR**	
4						
5				Mean	20.30%	
6				Minimum	16.46%	
7				Maximum	24.22%	
8				Standard Deviation	1.63%	
9				Mean+2 Standard deviations	23.56%	
10				Mean+3 Standard deviations	25.19%	
11				Mean-2 Standard deviations	17.03%	
12				Mean-3 Standard deviations	15.40%	
13				Range	7.76%	
14						
15						
16						

Figure 6.16: Results screen for risk analysis on IRR

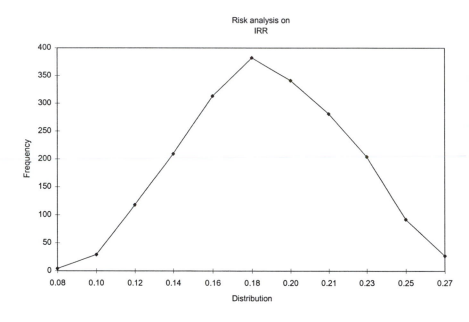

Figure 6.17: Graphical representation of risk analysis results for IRR

A different scenario can be seen by looking at Figures 6.18 and 6.19 which show the results of performing risk analysis on the NPV.

	A	B	C	D	E	F
1						
2						
3				Summary statistics for	NPV	
4						
5				Mean	8041.37	
6				Minimum	-55290.12	
7				Maximum	78835.48	
8				Standard Deviation	23296.24	
9				Mean+2 Standard deviations	54633.8447	
10				Mean+3 Standard deviations	77930.08	
11				Mean-2 Standard deviations	-38551.11	
12				Mean-3 Standard deviations	-61847.35	
13				Range	134125.59	
14						
15						
16						

Figure 6.18: Results screen for risk analysis on NPV

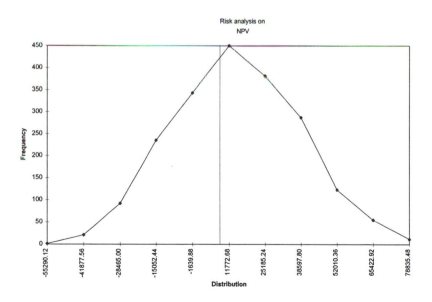

Figure 6.19: Graphical representation of risk analysis results on NPV

The example used to produce the results shown in Figures 6.18 and 6.19 would be regarded as a relatively high risk. The most likely outcome of this investment is an NPV of 470. Although this is in itself satisfactory, the investment also has the potential of making a substantial loss, i.e. as much as an NPV of -34,953. Of course if all goes well this investment could return a positive NPV of 32,598. This variability is the risk.

3.3 Choice of cost benefit modelling

The question of which of the above approaches would be most appropriate for a particular information systems investment is frequently raised.

In general risk analysis, as it delivers a much richer picture of the situation is wherever possible preferable. Unfortunately risk analysis is not used extensively in business, probably because of cultural assumptions that business and management issues are under the control of the organisation and are thus deterministic in nature. However with regards the other approaches to modelling, Figure 6.20 indicates the most suitable area of application.

Cost benefit approach	Application	Benefit
Cost displacement	Automation	Efficiency
Cost avoidance	Automation	Efficiency
Decision analysis	Information	Effectiveness
Impact analysis	Transformation	New business opportunity

Figure *6.20: Different benefit modelling approaches*

4. THE MERITS OF OUTCOME AND BENEFIT MODELLING

A considerable amount of work is required if information systems outcome and benefit modelling is to be undertaken successfully and if the results are to be of value. Therefore a basic question which has frequently been asked is:

Is the addition insight to be derived from information systems outcome and benefit modelling worth the effort?

In reality, unless some detailed modelling is done, management will not have much of an idea of what lies ahead, nor will it know how it is actually performing. Therefore, even though the estimation and the measurement of information systems performance is imperfect it is essential to produce these models to obtain some sort of indication of what the possible outcomes and benefits could be. However, whatever method or level of modelling is used and whatever metric is chosen be it financial or otherwise, it should be realised that it is likely to be no more than a subjective assessment of likely results with a low level of objectivity. This does not make the exercise invalid nor does it mean that it has no practical use. But it means that the results need to be used with care and sensitivity particularly to the assumptions underlying the models.

5. SUMMARY AND CONCLUSION

Without outcome and benefit modelling the best which can be achieved is an unclear view of what the information systems investment may achieve and how this will actually take place. To ensure that there is a clear understanding of how the investment will proceed and how the outcome and associated benefits will be generated it is essential to develop models at all three levels described in this chapter.

There are different degrees of outcome and benefit modelling. These include macro, meso and micro modelling. Within the micro modelling context there are also different types of cost benefit analysis which range from fairly simple single point estimate techniques to more sophisticated risk analysis. It is important to choose the appropriate level of sophistication and not to over work the detail or the numbers. In some cases, where the size of the investment is small, it may only be necessary to perform a general level of analysis.

The main reason why modelling is an important subject is that conceptual clarity regarding the impact of an information system investment on the business situation and on the financial resources of the organisation is important if a proposed application is to be authorised, successfully implemented and subsequently managed. Planning an information systems investment without performing a business modelling exercise is analogous to initiating a complex journey without consulting a map.

Benefit modelling is thus an important tool for the realisation of management desired outcomes of an investment. It can provide a rich picture of the possible results of the investment. But it is always important to remember the words of one of the greatest economists of this century, John Maynard Keynes (1953), who pointed out that, in the final analysis it is human *'motive or whim or sentiment or chance'* which tends to make the investment decisions and not the logic or mathematics of the model.

7

An ABR Programme

'There is nothing more difficult to take in hand, more perilous to conduct, or more uncertain in its success, than to take the lead in the introduction of a new order of things'

Nicolo Machiavelli, The Prince, 1532

1. INTRODUCTION

This chapter discusses the underlying principles of ABR. It considers a framework for the implementation of ABR through a suitable programme for information systems using the principles of continuous participative evaluation (Sherwood-Smith 1989; Finne *et al.* 1995).

A key issue in delivering better information system benefits is the paying of appropriate and continuous attention to the real business objectives of the information system. Once these business objectives and the implementation risks associated with them, have been clearly understood by all the information system's primary stakeholders, it is necessary to continuously track the objectives and the risks until the information system is delivered. There is also a need to clearly state how these goals relate to the corporate financial objectives and translate them into project management issues. Specific goals for all those involved in delivering the business benefits need to be defined and allocated to appropriate people. All of this is achieved while recognising the contingent nature of the information systems' development process which needs to allow for the possibility of goal-post changes.

Thus at the centre of the ABR approach is an understanding of the business objectives of information systems and how these can be realised by the range of stakeholders. A key aspect of ABR is the notion of continuous assessment and co-evolution. Care needs to be taken to ensure that as the project progresses the stakeholders' understanding of the business objective grows[1]. This requires that there should be a mutually sustained understanding of what the outcome of the information system will be and results in a process of continuous confirmation that the project is on track and that it will produce appropriate benefits.

This chapter addresses some of the issues involved in ABR which need to be developed and implemented if ABR is to be effectively used.

The chapter begins the discussion of the detail of the framework which is needed by the primary stakeholders including information systems executives, project managers, eventual users and consultants to improve the return on information systems investment. It discusses the major aspects of the procedures required for an ABR programme from the

---

[1] If a business objective should change during the software development life cycle this change needs to be fully considered, despite the danger of scope creep. Clearly scope creep is a lesser evil than information systems irrelevance due to changing requirements. Some organisations are so frightened by the prospect of scope creep that they strongly discourage any discussion of the information systems requirement as soon as the specification has been signed off. This completely denies the contingent nature of business activities.

information system conception until it is commissioned as a functioning system[2].

An ABR programme can make a major contribution to the successful implementation and subsequent management of information systems, and especially to the eventual acceptability of the information system to all its stakeholders. Furthermore, this will result in a greater acceptance of the vital importance of information systems by senior and top managers in all organisations as the twenty first century approaches.

A benefits realisation programme is essentially a process which brings together three groups of stakeholders whose input and collaboration are required for the successful co-evolution and use of an information system. It is sometimes useful to think of the use of an ABR programme as being similar to navigating a ship through an archipelago in such a way that the craft is aware of all the islands and is able to satisfy the requirement or vested interested of all these entities, including the crew while reaching an agreed destination.

There are three distinct phases to ABR. The first of these is referred to by the authors as *Setting the Course* which involves the development of sets of precise requirements under the headings of a *business picture*, a *financial picture* and a *project picture*. The second phase is the *Formative Evaluation* and involves closely assessing the progress of the project whilst phase three is called *Moving Forward* which provides a feedback loop which should be available, not only during development, but also throughout the entire life of the project.

---

[2] An ABR programme could in fact be of value throughout the life of the information system and not simply limited to the development phase of a system. However in this book the authors have focused on its use during the process of information system's development.

Thus this benefits programme is a reiterative process whereby a system's requirements are refined or co-evolved in a controlled manner. Figure 7.1 shows the reiterative nature of this activity.

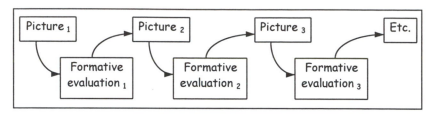

Figure 7.1: Reiterative process of an ABR programme

An ABR programme begins when the information system is first conceptualised and if correctly managed the process can continue to deliver improvements throughout the life of the information system.

2. PRINCIPLES OF CONTINUOUS PARTICIPATIVE EVALUATION

The ABR programme described in this chapter is based on the principles of formative evaluation or continuous participative evaluation for information systems. The process is grounded on six underlying philosophical propositions or principles[3] of information systems management which have been developed from notions of post-modern management which are:

---

[3] Philosophical principles are regarded for the purposes of this chapter as those that help set the framework in which information systems will be managed. This framework includes issues related to the ownership, the evaluation and the performance of information systems.

1. *Whether or not an information system succeeds is a function of management attitudes orientation and management processes rather than the application of the technology itself; there are no silver bullets or magic solutions; mechanistic solutions or processes such as the software development life cycle are increasingly unlikely to deliver satisfactory results; in addition back to basics programs are unlikely to succeed.*

2. *Information systems are not the property of the information systems department. Every system requires a stakeholder who is the user/owner. Information systems themselves do not deliver benefits but rather facilitate improvements to business performance in the hands of committed stakeholders. This being the case, information systems benefit delivery is the responsibility of the management who requested and commissioned the system. It is essential that these managers are the primary evaluators of the information system. Successful systems development needs the commitment of multiple stakeholders both multiple primary and multiple secondary stakeholders.*

3. *An information system's requirements evolve over time starting from the initial statement of the information system concept and will continue to evolve until the system is discontinued or scrapped; these changes in the information system's requirements may reflect changes in information technology, business requirements or environmental conditions or business growth; thus it is important that none of the stakeholders should be hostile to proposals to change; this does not mean that any proposed change need not be carefully justified.*

4. *An information system's actualisation is frequently a compromise[4] of the requirements of the various stakeholders; when these stakeholders have a common vision and shared values and are prepared to ensure the interests of their own personal domain are aligned with the interests of the organisation as a whole, satisfactory results will be achieved; thus the information leadership role needs to be defined in terms of the need to capture attention, create meaning and thus shared values, and building trust.*

5. *A phased delivery of systems as opposed to big bang delivery, tends to reduce risk of systems development failure and speed up the delivery of required business benefits; however phased delivery may require more work and thus be more expensive; although this approach may also allow some benefits to be realised sooner.*

6. *A process of continuous and dynamic evaluation and debate or dialogue between knowledgeable stakeholders recognising the need for a common vision and shared values, individual autonomy and the inevitable presence of ambiguity, provides the best chance for the optimisation of the benefits which may be derived with the assistance of information systems.*

---

[4] The word compromise is sometimes believed to have connotations of a settlement of competing interests which in fact satisfies none of the parties in contention. This meaning of the word is not intended here but rather the word is used to suggest that it is usually not possible to have all the facilities in a system which the user might like and that it is frequently in the organisation's best interests to deliver perhaps only 80% or so of the ideal information system's requirement. Sometimes stakeholders are unable to reach agreement and thus a compromise is not possible and higher levels of management have to be summoned to resolve disputes. If this is the case then care must to taken to manage such a situation with a light touch as forced agreements seldom hold for long and usually result in more disputes later. Information systems implementation may easily be spoiled or even wrecked by non-cooperation of the stakeholders and considerable effort needs to be expended in order to ensure that this does not happen.

The application of these principles leads to a non-traditional[5] approach to information systems conceptualisation and development as well as to the subsequent assessment of the effectiveness of the information system. In addition, through a high degree of openness or glasnost, which involves expecting information systems professionals to play a co-evolutionary role together with line managers and users, as well as financial staff, more effective information systems may be developed. This means that information systems need no longer be tied into single purpose-built developments created by technicians, but can be the product of collaboration. Central to this is an iterative, continuous participative evaluation process, supporting IS development and focusing on achievable benefits.

3. A BENEFITS REALISATION PROGRAMME THE PROCESS

Although it is not possible to be prescriptive about how an ABR programme will or should be conducted, it is possible to say that in general it consists of three distinct phases which may be described as

1. Setting the course by developing the three initial pictures

2. The formative evaluation process

3. Moving forward towards the objectives after closing of the feedback loop

---

[5] Traditionally information systems were developed by information systems people with only the minor involvement of line management or users during the systems' specification stage and perhaps during the systems' testing. Accounting and financial staff were occasionally invited to help prepare an ex-ante or summative evaluation of the investment as part of a feasibility study.

These phases are shown in Figure 7.2 and each will be discussed in detail in this chapter. In addition the process by which these phases operate to ensure focused professional information systems management will be explained.

The diagram in Figure 7.2 may be seen as a chart describing the route through which a successful information system's implementer needs to navigate or travel. At the outset the stakeholders need to clearly and comprehensively describe their business, financial and project objectives or requirements and provide a firm commitment to the project. This is not a trivial process and will require a considerable amount of time and the involvement of a number of stakeholders from each group. This ultimately leads to the authorisation of the project aimed at achieving these outcomes and the work commences.

Project management techniques are then used to control the day-to-day work. However, an ABR programme means that all those involved are sensitive to how the project is progressing and to whether or not it is possible to make improvements to either how the information system is being developed or to the actual business solution itself.

Formative evaluation sessions are held at regular planned intervals during which progress is reviewed. A key aspect of this review is the notion of continuous assessment and co-evolution as the stakeholders navigate towards an effective information system's solution to their business problem or opportunity. This means that as the project progresses the stakeholder's understanding of the business objectives and requirements grows, and thus there develops a mutually sustained understanding of what the outcome of the information system will be. This effectively requires that there is a process of continuous confirmation that the project is on track and that appropriate benefits will be realised.

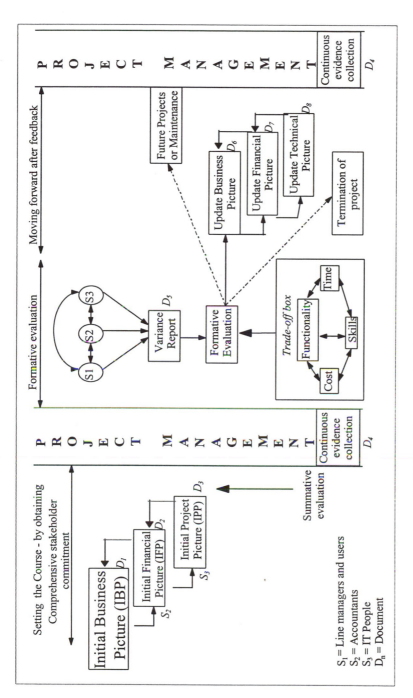

Figure 7.2: Methodology for formative evaluation

Figure 7.2 shows the three phases which will be discussed separately later in the chapter and in Chapters Eight and Nine. It also shows three sets of stakeholders who are described as line managers and users, accountants and IT people. Each of these groups produce their own picture of the information system's project. Each of these pictures is described as a document. Thus D_1 is the IBP and D_2 is the IFP and D_3 is the IPP. D_4 represents the continuous evidence collection documents. D_5 is the sum of D_1, D_2, D_3 and D_4 presented to the formative evaluation session. D_6, D_7 and D_8 are the updated business, financial and project pictures after each round of the formative evaluation process.

A formative evaluation session may determine that a project is on track and that no changes to the specification are required or it may suggest that substantial rethinking is needed, perhaps even project abandonment.

Thus an ABR programme using a formative evaluation technique is not a one off event, but rather a continuous process which is repeated periodically throughout the information systems development life cycle as well as beyond. This was illustrated in Figure 4.4 in Chapter Four. From Figure 4.4 it may be seen that an ABR programme, as defined in this chapter, is ideally suited to an environment in which prototyping is used, although it is also applicable to other approaches to information systems implementation.

Perhaps the single most important aspect of benefits realisation using a formative evaluation approach is the fact that it builds consensus among the various stakeholders by recognising their co-creation and co-evolutionary status in developing business solutions. Not only will this approach produce more information systems benefits, but it will also reduce waste. It will tend to decrease the amount of time it takes to deliver effective systems which help produce direct business benefits and thus substantially improve the utilisation of the organisation's resources.

4. SUMMATIVE EVALUATION

As may be seen from both Figure 7.2 and Figure 4.4 summative evaluation, which has been defined in Chapter Three, is also an important issue which needs to be understood when using an ABR programme.

The process of preparing the three initial pictures, especially the IFP, may be regarded as involving summative evaluation. The functions of summative evaluation are:

1. To help decide whether to invest in a particular information system;

2. To assist the capital rationing process in order to prioritise projects;

3. To learn if the investment was successful.

As mentioned before measurements of information systems evaluation approaches which focus on the above issues may be regarded as summative. Summative evaluation approaches typically aim at assessing outcomes and impacts; they take place either at the start of a project or towards the end or after its conclusion. This means that the results of such an evaluation may be used to consider whether an investment proposal should take place at all, to redirect investment efforts in the organisation towards opportunities affording a possible better return, or to convince others that a new set of investments are required.

In this ABR programme summative evaluation occurs at the outset. This is equivalent to a feasibility study or the development of a business case. Using ABR these evaluations will be regularly repeated until after the project has been implemented.

5. THE DEVELOPMENT OF THE THREE INITIAL PICTURES

During the first phase of the ABR programme the stakeholders are identified and comprehensive stakeholder commitment is obtained[6]. Also some form of summative evaluation, probably a feasibility study will be undertaken.

Each information system will have its own set of stakeholders, and precisely who these stakeholders are will depend upon the context of the information systems investment. Multiple stakeholders result in many different perspectives, some of which could be conflicting, which need to be accommodated if the information system is to be considered a success (Serafeimidis and Smithson 1995; Symons 1994). However it is probably useful to look at the stakeholders in terms of three principal generic groups. These are:

1. The line managers and user staff who will ultimately be responsible for making a success of the information system;

2. The accountants and financial officers who are responsible for ensuring the organisation's funds are suitably employed;

3. The information systems staff who will bring the technical expertise required to actually produce and/or purchase or assemble the information system.

---

[6] Without stakeholder commitment an information systems development project should not be commenced. Without an appropriate level of stakeholder commitment an information systems development will almost certainly fail. It is not always easy to obtain adequate stakeholder commitment and thus time and resources may have to be utilised to ensure that this occurs. Of course a problems can arise during an IS development project if some of the primary stakeholders change, either due to promotion, transfer, leaving the organisation or even death. This can cause a loss of support for the project and a re-evaluation needs to be made as to whether the information systems project is still required.

Each of the above three groups of stakeholders will have a view or sometimes a vision as to what the information system should achieve in order to help them attain their corporate goals. These views or visions are referred to as the Initial Business Picture (IBP) for the line managers and users, Initial Financial Picture (IFP) for the accountants and financial staff and the Initial Project Picture (IPP) for the information technology people[7].

Figure 7.3 shows phase one of the ABR programme which is the development of these three initial pictures. Each of these three views or visions are reduced to comprehensive statements which are referred to as pictures. The production of these pictures is an interactive process which may require a number of reiterations before they are finalised. For the purposes of an ABR programme these pictures are checklists of the issues which need to be addressed and agreed before an information systems development project can get under way.

6. SUMMARY AND CONCLUSION

ABR needs to be implemented through a benefits realisation programme using the principles of continuous participative evaluation. An ABR programme is a sophisticated process which is based on a series of six principles which rely on notions of post-modern management.

---

[7] Each of these different groups or sets of stakeholders may actually be headed up by a line manager. If this is the case he or she will be supported by technical people. To produce an IFP the skills of capital budgeting are required and to produce an IPP, a knowledge of the software development life cycle and a familiarity with project management techniques are needed. However such technical individuals may only be required to support line management decisions.

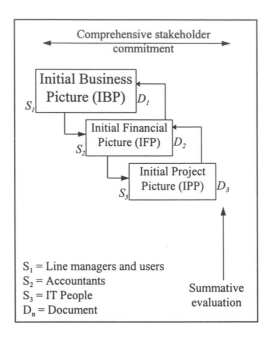

Figure 7.3: Setting the course by developing the three initial pictures

ABR requires the development of the three initial pictures, the business picture, the financial picture and the project picture. These pictures provide three different views of the proposed information systems development from the perspective of the eventual business users, the financial staff and the information systems professional.

The production of the pictures is an iterative process which is denoted by the backward flowing arrows in Figure 7.3.

The production of the three pictures is the first phase in the process of ABR and it is critical.

8

Developing the Initial Pictures

'Don't get involved in partial problems, but always take flight to where there is a free view over the whole single *great problem, even if this view is still not a clear one'*

Ludwig Wittgenstein, Notebooks 1914–1916, entry for 1 Nov. 1914 (ed. by Anscombe, 1961).

1. INTRODUCTION

The ABR programme described in this chapter is designed to be easy to use and relatively economical in terms of management time and evidence collection effort. However, the process suggests a mind-set shift on the part of management whereby stakeholders play a co-creation and a co-evolutionary role in the development of information systems in order to focus on business benefits rather than information technology. As development progresses all the principal stakeholders appreciate more fully the opportunities of the technology and the business problem, and guide the development process towards a system that delivers business benefits. The process complements the recognised and well understood project management and financial management techniques that are usually necessary to satisfy top management sponsorship of an information system, and subsequently successful information systems delivery.

2. THE PROCESS

The proposed ABR programme for information systems development is based on an iterative formative evaluation process.

This process consists of the following seven major activities which are illustrated in Figure 8.1.

1. Initialisation of project

2. Production of pictures

3. An agreement to proceed

4. System development

5. Evidence collection

6. Review and learning

7. Update of the pictures

8. Return to step 3.

The reiterative ABR process is based on the evaluation of progress, a review to ensure that the development is on course to realise business benefits, and an agreement to proceed. The reiteration continues until the project has been concluded.

The trigger for an information systems ABR programme is the appreciation by the organisation of a primary business problem or the vision of an opportunity which can be resolved, in the case of a problem, or enabled, in the case of an opportunity, by using information technology.

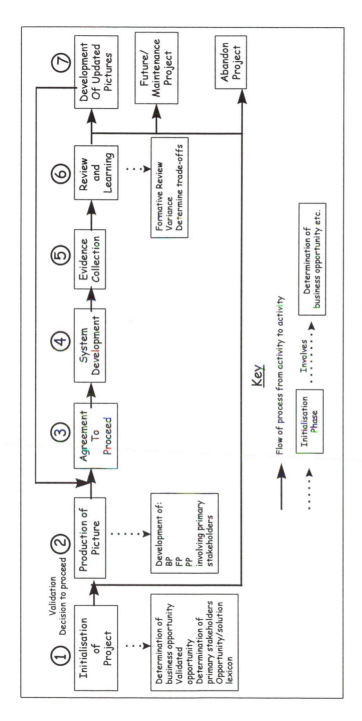

Figure 8.1: The process of ABR

This is the entry point into activity 1 *Initialisation of project*. A clear statement of the problem or the opportunity which the intended information system is planned to overcome or support is made. One of the primary objectives of the initialisation activity, once the problem or opportunity has been clearly stated, is to validate that the project is worth tackling.

Initialising the project involves gaining a clear understanding of the organisational objectives which are to be realised as a result of the information system development. In so doing the context for the information system development, as well as the goals and expected benefits of the proposed system, will become clear. The business opportunity is validated by ensuring that it is aligned to the strategy of the organisation as expressed by its critical success factors. The deliverable at the end of step 1 will be a document which will contain an authorisation to proceed with a detailed examination of the project. This document is not the final agreement to proceed with the actual project itself but only a first step.

The second step, activity 2 *Production of pictures*, requires the preparation of what is termed the Initial Business Picture (IBP) and two supporting pictures the Initial Financial Picture (IFP) and the Initial Project Picture (IPP), these are described in more detail later in this chapter. For the purpose of describing the process, these pictures can be viewed as a formalised expression of the information systems development project targets in business benefits terms, with the supporting financial budget and the supporting development project plans. Once the pictures have been prepared a key decision making point is reached. The pictures are a model of the business opportunity, the context, the financial impact of an information system and a project plan. The deliverable at the end of step 2 will be a document which will contain all the three pictures required for the management of the project.

Based on this information a decision can be made and activity 3 *An agreement to proceed*, can be completed.

Following the decision to go ahead, activity 4 *System development*, is commenced. Once a part of the information system has been developed some deliverables from development work exist. At first this may simply be a paper deliverable, an analysis report, but as systems development advances this may be a prototype and eventually will be the results of live testing of the system.

In activity 5 *Evidence collection*, the stakeholders familiarise themselves with the deliverable. If participation has been genuinely exercised then the stakeholders will be familiar with the deliverable. Evidence collection for senior management may take the form of reading a clearly expressed management summary.

In activity 6 *Review and learning*, the stakeholders review and evaluate progress. Progress is evaluated against the business, financial and project targets, with specific emphasis on business benefits and regulatory action, to ensure information systems development stays on course to deliver business benefits. The various tasks of the process are supported by specific techniques and the business stakeholders participate in the process, to ensure that business and not technological issues come to the fore.

The formative evaluation cycle is completed with activity 7 *Update of the pictures*. This activity can be viewed as equivalent to updating the budget in accounting terms. In this process some information systems development targets will be updated, but another key aspect of this process is that the stakeholders learn to understand better what is required and what is possible. The development process continues by returning to activity 3 with an agreement to proceed.

2.1 Picture initiation and development

A more comprehensive view of the process of initiating and preparing the first pictures is provided in Figure 8.2.

This process of ABR differs from traditional or standard information system's project management in that it focuses on the major business elements of the information systems project and ensures that the locus of responsibility is clearly focused on the primary stakeholders. As out of the group of primary stakeholders the eventual users are clearly the most affected or impacted by the system, it is essential that they take ownership of the project ab initio. This ownership requires a high degree of involvement and commitment from the user (Lodge 1989) and unless this is forthcoming the information systems development faces a high probability of failure.

The initiator[1] launches the project by identifying a primary business problem or describing a primary business opportunity and reducing this to a statement. The project is initiated (Initialisation of Project) by formalising the problem or opportunity statement and validating that the project is worthwhile. As part of the initialisation an agreement is reached as to who should be involved in the development of this information system (Terms of Reference/Participation).

Because formative evaluation is significantly influenced by the profile of the participants, the identification of the stakeholders, their willingness to participate and the consequent make up of the project and review teams is a key issue for this process. Once agreement is reached requests to the stakeholders to participate can be issued and the terms of reference for the project stated.

---

[1] Although the authors recognise that any stakeholder could actually be an initiator, they believe that from the commencement of the work on the prospective project, an eventual user needs to take on or take over the role of the initiator.

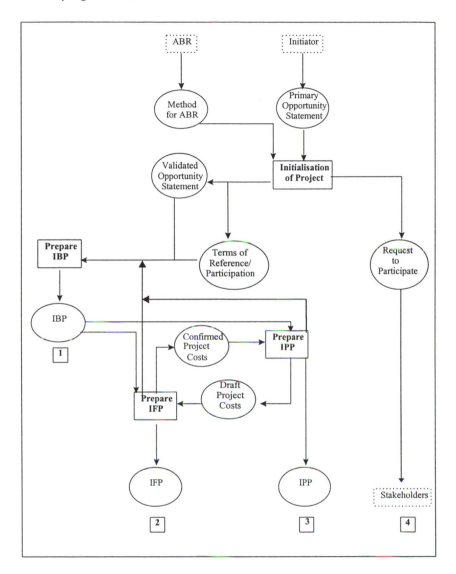

Figure 8.2: The initiation and creation of the pictures

Over the life of the information system the stakeholders will change and evolve. This is catered for in this process. Note how the IFP and the IPP require considerable dialogue and interaction between the financial and technical staff because the technical issues has direct impact on the financial estimates and the funding available in turn has a direct effect on the type of technical solutions which may be proposed.

3. THE PICTURES

The ABR process or programme has two key characteristics. The first is the process which is based on an active participative evaluation and learning paradigm. The second characteristic is the representation of the primary issues to be understood and monitored as pictures. These pictures are statements, models in a loose sense, of the context, the required benefits and the specification of the appropriate metrics to be used to evaluate, monitor and control benefits realisation. The terminology set used in this approach is the Business Picture (BP), the Financial Picture (FP) and the Project Picture (PP). The systematic, and holistic use of the BP, the FP and the PP enables effective planning, evaluation and control of the systems development progress and thus ensures the appropriate benefits realisation from the information system investment. In this chapter the authors address the issue of the preparation of the BP in much more detail than either the FP or the PP. There are two reasons for this. Firstly the BP is the cornerstone on which the FP and the PP are actually built and if the preparation of the BP is not undertaken correctly the subsequent work will certainly be flawed. Secondly although not many organisations actually prepare a document which has any resemblance to a BP the opposite is true for the FP and the PP. FP and PP type documents are used by many organisations in an attempt to plan and control their information systems development activities.

Some items on the pictures are simply a statement of a contextual situation or a target which the system development is expected to achieve. Other items are numbers and some may be graphical representations. They are represented in these pictures in a summary form. These high level statements will be underpinned by detailed information which will support the picture.

Once the three pictures have been produced, a decision is made and an agreement reached as to whether or not to launch the project. Figure 8.3 shows the process of preparing the Business Picture. Note that there is a particular order in which the picture should be developed which corresponds to the traditional logic of information systems development and follows the order in which the items are listed in Figure 8.4.

The first logical grouping which is displayed in the first column (C1) in Figure 8.3 describes the activities required to validate the business problem or opportunity and to establish the primary stakeholders and record the key words in the solution lexicon. These activities effectively set the terms of reference. The second column (C2) describes how the terms of reference extend to include a statement of the required outcome and a note of the alternative solutions reviewed. The third set of activities in the next column (C3) describe the chosen solution, the rationale for choosing this particular solution and who the solution champion will be. The fourth column (C4) shows how the activities associated with the identification of the benefits, their timing (Daniels 1994), and the creation of the various matrices are logically grouped. Tangible and intangible benefits need to be specified (Hogbin and Thomas 1994). This section also includes the key performance indicators which are associated with the critical success factors. Finally column five (C5) groups the issues related to risk as well as the ideal term report.

The FP and the PP do not need to follow the same strict logical sequence. Much more flexibility is available in the production of these pictures. Nonetheless the order in which the items are listed in Figures 8.12 and 8.17 are useful to follow.

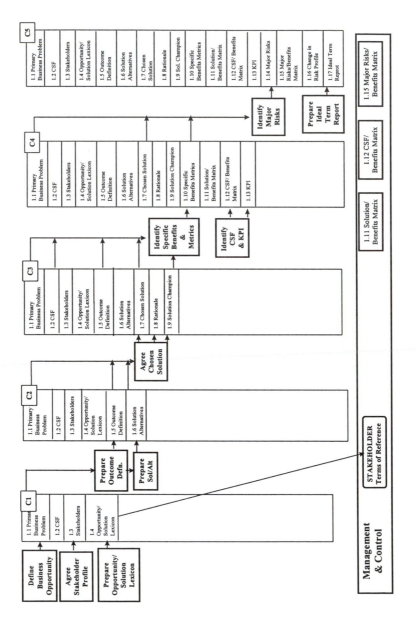

Figure 8.3: Activities required to validate the project

4. THE BUSINESS PICTURE (BP)

Figure 8.4 lists the issues which need to be addressed in the BP. These issues definitively describe the business opportunity and its context, why it is important to the organisation, who is responsible for it, what benefits it will deliver for whom and what risks it may encounter. In fact the BP may be regarded as a comprehensive business case for the project.

Item	Business issues
1.1	Primary business problem or opportunity
1.2	Critical success factors
1.3	Stakeholders
1.4	Opportunity/solution lexicon
1.5	Outcome definition
1.6	Solution alternatives
1.7	Chosen solution
1.8	Rationale
1.9	Solution champion
1.10	Specific benefits and metrics
1.11	Stakeholder-benefits matrix
1.12	Critical success factor-benefits matrix
1.13	Key performance indicators
1.14	Major risks
1.15	Major risks-benefits matrix
1.16	Change in risk profile
1.17	Ideal term report

Figure 8.4: Business Picture (BP)

4.1 Primary business problem or opportunity

Item 1.1 in the BP expresses the opportunity or the problem which the organisation faces. It is a succinct statement and/or list of problems being addressed by the proposed information systems initiative[2]. An example of a problem stated clearly and simply might be 'Gross sales invoice value too small to provide the required return on investment'.

The statement of the primary business problem or opportunity may be the most important issue for the entire project. If the primary business problem or opportunity is not correctly understood the resulting information system will probably be of little value. This has been identified by Davenport (1993) when writing of process innovation Davenport:

> 'the clarity with which the mission of process re-design is set is a critical success factor for the project.'

The primary business problem or opportunity is usually identified by one stakeholder who is frequently a member of line management. The validity of this proposed problem or opportunity needs to be confirmed or validated by canvassing the opinions of other interested groups in the organisation and by ensuring that it clearly supports the current strategic objectives of the organisation expressed through its current mission statement, organisational objectives and business strategy. It is important that senior management participate at this stage in the validation of the proposed information systems opportunity as if they are not represented it may transpire that they have quite a different view of the opportunity or problem and the suggested

---

[2] Although it is useful to keep this statement relatively short, it is sometimes beneficial to explicitly state the business assumptions that are behind the business problem or opportunity.

information systems project could be irrelevant and thus subsequently vetoed.

The amount of work which will be conducted and the techniques used for an opportunity validation will be directly a function of the size and complexity of the project. If the proposal is relatively small, either in terms of costs or other resource allocation, then the proposal may be validated by simply referring to the organisation's explicit or implicit strategy and critical success factors. If on the other hand the proposal is for a larger system then there are a set of major techniques available which include strategic alignment testing, brainstorming or even benchmarking.

The cost of this exercise could be substantial but it is clearly an essential investment if spurious or even irrelevant projects are to be avoided.

4.2 Critical success factors (CSF)

Item 1.2 of the BP, which is entered at the initialisation stage of the project, lists the key CSFs for the business or organisation which are being addressed by the information system development. There are several different ways of using CSFs and in this context they are employed to check on the relevance of the proposed system and to help identify the possible associated benefits.

Critical success factors are derived from the organisation's mission, objectives, goals and corporate strategy. Thus if the organisation is a cost leader then a CSF will probably be, for example, to reduce the cost of administration.

To deliver maximum benefits for the organisation the information system needs to be aligned to one or more of the organisation's CSFs. For example, if one of the critical success factors for the business is to reduce costs by changing the customer profile from having many small, low value, customers to having a smaller number of large high value customers, then one of the business benefits of the information system which addresses this could be to have 'higher average invoice value'. So this item stems from the stated CSFs of the organisation and identifies a way of achieving this supported by the information system.

CSFs may have been prepared for the organisation during its routine planning procedures but if this has not been the case, time needs to spent on this issue as it is a major technique for assisting in the validation of information systems opportunities.

4.3 Stakeholders

Item 1.3 is a list of the primary stakeholders in the project. At the more detailed level, the backing sheets for this item are job descriptions specifying the role of the particular stakeholder in the project and the responsibilities of each stakeholder in the context of the project.

Agreeing this item in the BP is not a trivial task and in fact it is central to the ABR approach. A benefits realisation programme needs to be participative and for that the role of the participants must be agreed. One of the key critical success factors for the ABR process is that all the principal stakeholders be correctly identified. Formative evaluation is significantly influenced by the profile of the participants, the identification of the stakeholders, their willingness to participate and the consequent make up of the project and review teams. Once agreement is reached, requests to the stakeholders to participate can be issued and the terms of reference for the project stated. These stakeholders should not only be committed to an environment of learning and understanding (Walsham 1993), but should also have the time to be continually involved in the development of the system.

The selected stakeholders should be competent, should share the same values for the information systems' success, should ideally not be antagonistic to other stakeholders' interests and the participating group should be balanced. The purpose of involving various groups of stakeholders has several objectives. The first is to ensure a better understanding of the business problem or opportunity and the technological solution. A better understanding is achieved through the learning process which enhances the competence of the participants. Thus the selection of knowledgeable and competent people to participate in the project will influence its success.

Three sets of primary or core stakeholders are recognised. These are line managers and end users who ultimately have the responsibility for making the system succeed; accountants and financial officers who are responsible for ensuring the investment of the organisation's resources are controlled in terms of corporate policy, and the IT people who bring technical expertise to information systems development and subsequent management.

Secondary stakeholders may also be involved and may from time to time include vendors, clients, auditors to mention only three.

The make up or composition of the stakeholder group may evolve over the life of a project. In the process of review and learning new stakeholders may be included and their roles and responsibilities for the project defined on an ongoing basis.

4. Opportunity/solution lexicon

Item 1.4 is a list of key terms and definitions which will be used when communicating about the information systems project and the business benefits opportunity presented by the project. It is presented as a lexicon/glossary[3] and in many cases it will not be a lengthy document. Having defined the terms ensures that all the stakeholders are using the same language when they are discussing the opportunity and its possible solution. This is similar to the definition of terms described by Checkland (1986).

5. Outcome definition

Item 1.5 is a statement or a list of the expected results in precise business terms of the information systems initiative. It relates to the primary business problem or opportunity and represents in concrete terms the vision of how the opportunity will be realised. It is derived directly from the primary business problem or opportunity statement given in point 1.1 of the picture. So, for example, if the information system is targeted at changing the profile of the company's customer base from having many small customers to a more restricted group of large highly credit worthy customers then the hoped for outcome can be expressed as: more sales revenues on fewer invoices from well established customers of good financial standing who pay promptly. Another expected outcome could be that the business relationship with the customer will be much tighter and that the salesperson will call much more frequently on the customer and spend more time with them.

---

[3] The authors have avoided the term dictionary or repository as they would imply a much more comprehensive approach to this lexicon than is actually required. The purpose of the lexicon is simply to check that all the stakeholders are using the same meanings for the same words.

It is important for the outcome statement to be comprehensive and thus carefully thought through. A brainstorming session is a useful way of tackling this issue.

4.6 Solution alternatives

Item 1.6 is a summary of the solutions which have been considered. The item at this level in the BP will be represented as a summary statement for each of the alternatives considered. For example, if the business opportunity was as outlined above, a shift of emphasis towards larger more closely tied customers and more frequent sales calls, then various information systems alternatives might be considered. The solution might be a quite straightforward one based on the redesign of sales information reports for salesmen using the current information system and technology. Alternatives might be to install a telecommunications link to salespersons' homes and direct the sales operation in a more focused way. Another might be to arrange electronic mail exchanges with customers in order to be more responsive to customer needs and tie them in to the company.

The summary statements on the BP will be the result of some business analysis performed by information systems or business analysis professionals using recognised techniques. At this stage in the project the analysis will be at feasibility study level and, as mentioned above, carried out by experts so that no significant delay will be built into the preparation of the initial BP. Nevertheless analysing and summarising alternatives is a significant task. The summary item will be supported by some form of analysis report.

The importance of this item on the BP is that it shows what alternatives have been considered so that if some stakeholder subsequently comes up with a new slant then it can be recognised as such, new and never considered before, and discussed in that light.

4.7 Chosen solution

Item 1.7 is a summary description of the chosen solution. The task of preparing the chosen solution will involve some systems analysis and design work by information systems or business analysis professionals. This work is complementary to the work of looking at solution alternatives above and is a more detailed description of the chosen solution.

At this stage in the project the description of the chosen solution is still at a relatively high level and not over technical. It is aimed at being understood by all the stakeholders. The summary item on the BP will be supported by some form of design report. The techniques that support this activity are the recognised systems analysis and design techniques of information systems development.

4.8 Rationale

Item 1.8 gives the rationale for the chosen solution. The importance of this item in the BP is that it records the decision for a specific solution. It records why the decision was made at that time and by whom, so as to avoid going over old ground in future steps of the project. If a new route is taken at some future date then the new decision is made knowing explicitly what went before.

4.9 Solution champion

Item 1.9 supports item 1.7 of the picture. It recognises that information systems solutions to business problems are more likely to succeed if the solution is championed by a line manager. This item records who the champion of the chosen solution is. If there is no champion for the chosen solution then the information systems development is unlikely to realise business benefits.

4.10 Specific benefits and metrics

Item 1.10 is derived from the outcome definitions specified in item 1.5 of the business picture, and the chosen solution. It identifies the specific benefits which the chosen solution will deliver in business terms. These benefits will not be stated here in financial terms, as financial estimates will be produced for the FP.

Business benefits will be stated in terms of the effect of the system. Thus a sales order process system could have business benefits attributed to it such as those described under meso or intermediate models in Chapter Five.

For benefits to be achieved they need to be measurable[4], i.e. a stakeholder should be able to assess whether they have been delivered. Thus it is necessary to establish metrics which may be associated with any benefits that have been specified as possibly stemming from the information systems investment. This will allow an objective assessment to be made of the extent to which the information system has delivered the benefits.

---

[4] Virtually all information systems benefits are measurable, even intangible ones (Remenyi *et al.* 1995).

The primary benefits of some systems will essentially be simple functional requirements which will either exist or not exist. Such benefits will be evaluated on a yes/no binary scale. Others will be qualitative benefits that can only be evaluated on a qualitative scale (very good, good, satisfactory, poor, very poor). Finally some benefits will be measurable on an agreed numeric scale. For example, 'Average Invoice Value' can be measured on a £ per Invoice scale and a target set to define a satisfactory business benefit result from the information system development project

Identified benefit needs to be assigned a specific measurement metric so as to ascertain whether or not the benefit has been realised and this has been demonstrated in Figure 5.2 in Chapter Five.

4.11 Stakeholder-benefits matrix

The stakeholder-benefits matrix in item 1.11 represents in a matrix all the anticipated benefits and identifies which individual stakeholders are expected to profit from the implementation of each different aspect of the proposed information system.

This is an important item of the BP as it allows stakeholders to identify with the targeted benefits of the information system development. Another important facet of this report is that if the benefit analysis is incomplete it will draw this to the stakeholders' attention and this may allow refocusing on a more comprehensive statement of possible benefits. It will also identify stakeholders with no benefits accruing from the information system development, which may mean that they have been mistakenly included as primary stakeholders. An example of a stakeholder-benefit matrix is shown in Figure 8.6.

1.11	Stakeholder- benefits matrix		B1	B2	B3	B4	B5
		S1	*	*	*	*	
		S2			*	*	*
		S3		*	*		

Figure 8.6: Stakeholder-benefit matrix

In the above matrix the stakeholders are listed vertically and five different types of benefits may be associated with each stakeholder category. Of course both the number of rows and columns in this matrix may be expanded if it is so required. From Figure 8.6 it may be seen that stakeholder 1 is anticipating four distinctly different benefit types, whereas stakeholder three is only involved in two benefit types. The same matrix shows that it is anticipated benefit 3 will deliver utility to all three stakeholders, whereas benefit 1 and benefit 5 each impact only one category of stakeholder.

4.12 Critical success factors-benefits matrix

Item 1.12 is a matrix of all the anticipated business benefits accruing from the information system's development and identifies which corporate CSFs are supported by that benefit. This is an important control exercise for the realisation of relevant business benefits and for ensuring that the information system's development is to some extent strategically aligned. If an anticipated business benefit does not support a corporate CSF then it may not be a benefit at all or at least one of low priority. On the other hand if some relevant identified CSFs are not supported by any business benefits of the information system, then it is possible that the information system development is not adequately targeted. An example of a CSF/Benefit Matrix is supplied in Figure 8.7.

1.12	Critical success factor - benefits matrix.		B1	B2	B3	B4	B5
		CSF1	*			*	*
		CSF2	*	*		*	*
		CSF3		*	*		*
		CSF4			*		
		CSF5			*	*	*

Figure 8.7: CSF-benefit matrix

In the above matrix the CSFs are listed vertically and five different types of benefits may be associated with each CSF category. As with the stakeholder-benefit matrix both the number of rows and columns in this matrix may be expanded if it is so required. From Figure 8.7 it may be seen that benefit 5 has an impact on 4 out of 5 of the organisation's CSFs, whereas benefit 1 and benefit 2 only affects 2 of these CSFs. Similarly Figure 8.8 shows how CSF 2 will be enhanced by benefits 1, 2, 4 and 5, whereas CSF 4 will only be affected by benefit 3.

4.13 Key performance indicators

Item 1.13 lists all the Key Performance Indicators (KPI) associated with the declared CSFs. The listing of the KPIs support the identification of specific benefits and metrics. In fact the KPIs suggest the nature of the metric to be used with each type of benefit.

4.14 Major risks

Item 1.14 lists the major risks involved with the information system development. Its importance as an item on the BP in that any change involves moving towards a new situation and a new situation is open to risk. The major risks to the non realisation of business benefits and to the negative impacts of the information system development are listed so that they can be evaluated as acceptable or otherwise by the stakeholders. They can also be monitored during the development of the information system and re-evaluated. By making them part of the BP they are explicitly evaluated.

Risk is a challenging concept to define, understand and ultimately to manage, primarily because risk often means different things to different people. Historically risk is defined as the possibility that the eventual or actual input variables and the outcomes may vary from those originally estimated (Correia *et al.* 1989).

The management of risk is often a highly intuitive art (Turner 1995) and it is interesting to consider how McFarlan (1990) views some the risks associated with information systems. He suggests that there are two main categories of risk, which are described as risks associated with failures of execution and risks caused by failures of conceptualisation. McFarlan's views are expressed as a matrix in Figure 8.8 below and may be used as a supporting document to the BP.

4.14.1 Risk associated with failures of execution

The risk associated with failures of execution can be categorised under three headings. These are the risks related to the structuredness of a project, the degree to which a project incorporates company-specific technology, and the size of the project. It is possible to use a two by two matrix to position the different levels of risk relative to the dimensions of structuredness of the project and novelty of the technology. Such a matrix appears in Figure 8.8.

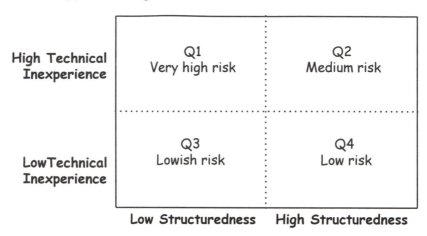

Figure 8.8: Matrix showing different degrees of risk
(Source: McFarlan 1990)

4.14.2 Risk implications

It may be said that there are ten information systems implementation risks and these are illustrated in Figure 8.9.

• It will never be delivered	• It will be delivered late
• It will exceed its budget	• It will lack functionality
• It will contain errors	• It will not be usable
• The IS will fail during operation	• It will be too difficult to enhance
• It will be too costly to support	• It will not perform to required standards

Figure 8.9: Some of the risks associated with an IS project

Although the above table is not definitive, it provides an excellent example of the number of IT risks which an organisation faces when implementing a new information system and may be used as a supporting document to the Major risks-benefit matrix required in the BP. It is crucial that the organisation identify and manage all of the risks associated with a potential project so as to increase the chance of success. The organisation thus needs to instigate a risk management process which entails the identification, evaluation and control of IT risks being faced in order to minimise the losses that could adversely affect it as a result of systems development activities (Berny and Townsend 1993).

4.15 Major risks-benefits matrix

Item 1.15 is a control item. The major risks are matched in a matrix representation to the business benefits so that stakeholders can ensure that major risks are not being taken for small benefits. By using the risk-benefits matrix and the stakeholders-benefits matrix together a balanced view can be taken by the stakeholders of the risks they are taking in the information systems development exercise and they can explicitly evaluate this. An example of a major risk-benefit matrix is supplied in Figure 8.10.

1.15	Major risks-benefits matrix		B1	B2	B3	B4	B5
		R1		*		*	*
		R2	*	*	*	*	*
		R3	*	*	*		*
		R4			*		*
		R5			*		*

Figure 8.10: Major risks-benefit matrix

In the above matrix the major risks are listed vertically and five different types of benefits may be associated with each major risk category. Of course both the number of rows and columns in this matrix may be expanded if it is so required. From Figure 8.10 it may be seen that risk 2 impacts all 5 potential benefits and thus deserves very special attention, whereas risk 4 and risk 5 only affect benefits 3 and 5.

4.16 Change in risk profile

Item 1.16 is not used in preparing the initial BP. It is used in the review process and expresses through a set of precise statements any major changes in the identified risks as stated in item 1.14 of the picture. It is highlighted as a separate issue for consideration because of the importance of changes in the risk profile of the information systems project.

4.17 Ideal term report

This last item, 1.17 in the BP, is essentially a series of statements expressing the ideal situation which the organisation hopes to realise in terms of the information systems development project. This is to be expressed primarily in business and organisational terms. The ideal term report serves to provide the preferred outcome to the question or questions posed by the business problem or opportunity described in item 1.1 of the picture. Figure 8.11 illustrates some concise statements which an organisation may hope to realise once the information systems has been operationalised for a period of time, for example one year.

1.	Within one year of the commissioning of the systems the sales revenues have increased by 20%, while
2.	reducing the number of clients.
3.	The average value per invoice has increased by at least 20%.
4.	There are fewer bad debts both in absolute terms and as a percentage of sales.
5.	Sales managers and representatives claim that the system has played a major role in achieving the above.
6.	Sales managers and representatives claim that they find the systems easy to use.
7.	There is a growing feeling among the sales staff at all levels that information systems can play a major role in helping them do a more efficient and more effective job.

Figure 8.11: An example of an ideal term report

The ideal term report is thus a set of succinct statements or a list of goals and business benefits which the organisation hopes to realise as a result of the information systems initiative.

5. THE FINANCIAL PICTURE (FP)

Figure 8.12 lists the issues which need to be addressed in the FP. This statement shows in money terms the benefits and costs of the project and includes some financial ratios which need to be evaluated and monitored to help ensure the financial health of the project. These financial ratios are, at the outset of the project, a predictive evaluation of the information systems project.

The FP includes the recognised cost categories for financial planning in information systems development and in many cases relies on the current financial planning and control system of the organisation. It also contains a comprehensive list of benefits.

Item	Financial issues
2.1	Project title
2.2	Project duration
2.3	Hardware costs
2.4	Software costs
2.5	Data communications costs
2.6	People costs
2.7	Commissioning costs
2.8	Group productivity tools
2.9	Individual or personal productivity tools
2.10	Informate the organisation
2.11	Reduce time and space in business processes
2.12	Create a corporate memory
2.13	Bind the organisation closely with clients and suppliers
2.14	Induce discontinuities by BPR
2.15	Required payback
2.16	Required return on investment
2.17	Required net present value
2.18	Major financial risks
2.19	Cost or benefit estimate changes since last review
2.20	Change in risk profile

Figure 8.12: The Financial Picture (FP)

5.1 Systems costs

Items 2.1 and 2.2 of the initial FP are simple statements of the name of the project and its anticipated duration.

The next five items from 2.3 to 2.7 are the estimated capital cost of the hardware, software, data, communications, people costs and commissioning costs. It is common practice to supply these forecasts as single point estimates. It is hoped that these costs will be reasonably accurate, i.e. within about 10% of the final costs. If there is a high degree of uncertainty about these cost estimate numbers then, instead of supplying single point estimates range values may be used and a process of risk analysis may be employed to perform the subsequent calculations. This was discussed in more detail in Chapter Six.

It is important to note that only the summary will be included in the FP. The detailed financial information will be available in the form of detailed budgets and costings within the organisation's accounting system. Of course the ABR process proposed here does not prescribe the accounting conventions to be used. The FP complements the current financial controls of the organisation. The user organisation will follow its own particular accounting conventions and may produce a statement similar to Figure 8.13. The FP formulated here suggests the issues which should be addressed to maintain an overall view of the financial status of the project.

5.2 Systems benefits

The initial FP provides a list of the major tangible benefits which may be derived from an information systems. These are listed from item 2.8 to 2.14 and these need to be addressed individually. It is important to state that in the FP there will be only summary figures quoted but these will, of course, be supported by detailed financial models.

5.2.1 Group productivity tools

Group productivity tools referenced in item 2.8 refer to any information systems which will increase the efficiency of all or a part of the organisation. Most automate systems will fall into this category. The basis of the estimation of the benefits to be derived from this type of application is that of cost displacement or cost avoidance. This usually involves comparing savings which are often related to the reduction in the number of staff required or a reduction of the scale of asset holding required, to the cost of the acquisition and the operation of the technology. The benefit modelling required here is well known to accountants and is frequently practised in organisations. This type of analysis is usually performed on a departmental or divisional basis.

In the BP the benefits to be derived from this category of application will already have been listed as business issues. In the FP an attempt will be made to quantify these benefits in monetary terms. At this stage the accuracy of these figures should not be an overwhelming concern but rather the figures should be seen as indications or rough estimates of the magnitude of cost and benefits.

It is not a trivial task to prepare a financial statement such as the one shown in Figure 8.13. The preparation requires an understanding of how the information system will be used and how this use will impact the requirement for resources in the organisation. Thus some benefit modelling needs to be undertaken during the process of creating the FP. It is important that the financial number used in this statement represent marginal costs and benefits.

Cost displacement statement	
Investment costs	
Hardware	1900
Software	2200
Communications	750
Commissioning	150
Total start up cost	5000
On-going costs	
Maintenance	300
People	150
Consumables	120
Accommodation	50
Total operating expenses	620
Estimated benefits	
Staff no longer required	950
Office expenses	450
Reduction in finance charges due to capital release	550
	1950
Net benefit	1330
ROI	0.266
Payback	4

Figure 8.13: A typical cost displacement statement

5.2.2 Individual or personal productivity tools

The individual or personal productivity tools referenced in item 2.9 impact the quantity and quality of the work of individuals. Sometimes this impact is sufficient to allow one person to do the work of several people and in such cases the calculation of the benefit is relatively straightforward and requires the same type of benefit modelling as described for group productivity tools. The problem which arises here is if the benefits are attributed to improvements in quality of work. In such cases an intangible benefit is under consideration and management judgement will need to be applied to arrive at an estimate of its magnitude. This type of benefit modelling often requires benefit values to be negotiated.

5.2.3 *Informate the organisation*

Item 2.10, informate the organisation (Zuboff 1988), refers to benefits associated with superior decision making and thus better performance due to individuals having more complete information about the circumstances of the organisation at their disposal. An information-decision making model may be constructed which will facilitate benefit modelling in this incidence and such a model was shown in Figure 6.5 in Chapter Six.

This model shows how information provided at the correct place, at the correct time and of the correct quality may lead to decisions. If these decisions are made appropriately and effectively they will produce actions and if executed efficiently and effectively will produce results. The is only the first step in benefit modelling which describes how the informate process works. When this has been agreed the primary stakeholders will then have to reduce the outcome of the improved information to financial figures and produce a statement similar to the one shown in Figure 8.13. As stated above this is not a trivial task and the preparation of these figures requires an understanding of how the information system will be used and how this use will impact the requirement for resources in the organisation. Typically more demanding benefit modelling needs to be undertaken for these types of benefits.

5.2.4 *Reduce time and space in business processes*

Item 2.11 is concerned with the reduction of time and space in business processes. This may lead to extensive benefits, many of which may be quantified in the same way as referred to above. In this case costs may be reduced by releasing office and/or factory space. Furthermore costs may be reduced or sales increased by more time being made available. These benefits have been discussed and supporting data supplied by Stalk and Hout (1990) show dramatic improvements in performance of organisations which improve their time cycles.

5.2.5 Create a corporate memory

Item 2.12 refers to creating a corporate memory which means that individuals may be empowered to perform tasks requiring greater skills than they would otherwise be able to undertake. This can open opportunities for more revenue or it may allow costs to be contained. In either case the benefit modelling approach will not be dissimilar to that described above.

5.2.6 Bind the organisation closely with clients and suppliers

Item 2.13 refers to binding the organisation closely with clients and suppliers through the use of inter-organisational systems such as EDI. These systems have a wide range of benefits which include the reduction of costs as well as increased opportunities for more revenue making activities. Relatively straightforward business modelling will be sufficient to forecast these benefits.

5.2.7 Induce discontinuities by business process reengineering

Item 2.14 looks at how information systems may be used to induce discontinuities by the application of business process re-engineering ideas. Once again this type of activity may either reduce costs or increase opportunities for more revenue making activities, or in fact both of these. Relatively straightforward business modelling will be sufficient to forecast these benefits.

5.3 Required payback, return on investment and net present value

Items 2.15, 2.16 and 2.17 of the FP refer to three classical measures of investment performance. These three statistics, payback, return on investment and net present value, are only examples of a much wider range of financial measures which may be used by accountants to assess the viability of an investment (Schall and Haley 1991; Brigham and Gapenski 1994; Drury 1995; Turner 1995). These figures need to be used with caution because they are highly dependent on the assumptions which have been used in their calculation. A graphical representation of these figures is often regarded as helpful and this is shown in Figure 8.16.

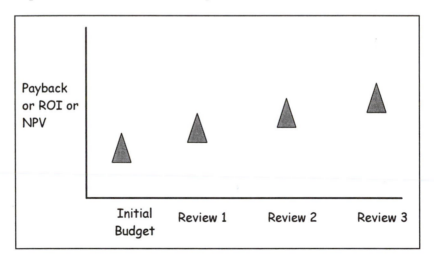

Figure 8.16: Graphical presentation of financial ratios

The *y* axis may be either Payback, ROI or Net Present Value and the graph tracks the latest best estimate, so that the trends can be appreciated in a global sense.

5.4 Major financial risks

The major financial risks, as referenced in item 2.18, which an information systems development project could face are related to escalation in the prices of the various inputs to the project. Thus the estimates for the hardware costs, the software costs, the data communications costs, the people costs and the commissioning costs are all potential risk points.

If elements of the system are being imported from a different currency area then the foreign exchange rate constitutes a potential risk area, as does the interest rate if the project is being financed out of borrowed funds.

5.5 Completing the FP

The last two items in the FP, 2.19 and 2.20, are the cost or benefit estimate changes since last review and the change in risk profile. Both of these are routine items which require regular recording to ensure that they do not drift too far from the original plan.

6. THE PROJECT PICTURE (PP)

In order to satisfactorily complete the PP it is necessary to apply the skills and techniques of project management.

6.1 Project management

It is at the PP level that the ABR process requires the most detail. Having established clear business problems or opportunities and having validated their appropriateness it is necessary for the information systems specialists to reduce these objectives to one or more deliverable products. In the case of ABR these software products which are defined in the project picture will represent actual application systems rather than the business solutions or outcomes which are defined in the business picture. Thus an entirely new level of detail is introduced here (Bradley 1996). It is important to note that operations manuals as well as training material are usually included in the definition of software products.

However, the concept of a software products is too general for the purposes of specific project planning and control and thus the activities required and the sequence in which they are needed in order to produce these products have to be defined.

Each activity then needs to be defined in terms of the traditional project management dimensions of resources and costs, as well as time and quality. However activities may also be seen in terms of management, technical and quality tasks. All the resources whether they be people, equipment or software products required and their availability need to be clearly defined at this stage in order to be able to produce the necessary plans.

Having specified the above an organisational structure needs to be put in place which defines different levels of responsibilities as well as the essential roles and responsibilities of the individuals involved in the project.

A project manager needs to be identified as early as possible in this process. In the ABR context the project manager will report directly to the solution champion who will act as the representative of the primary stakeholders. The primary stakeholders are equivalent to the project board. In the case of large projects a project support office may be required.

As a result of defining the activities and establishing the duration in which they are required to be completed as well as their ordering or sequencing the project manager can produce a task network and calculate a critical path. Once the resources required and the individual work roles have been determined, Gantt charts may be produced.

Project monitoring, reporting and control are built into the formative evaluation process and are thus integral to the ABR method.

6.2 Project Picture detail

Figure 8.17 lists the issues which need to be addressed in the PP. The PP highlights for the primary stakeholders and project management the key project planning issues for an information systems development project. The PP by itself is not a substitute for a comprehensive project plan, which is of course the sole responsibility of the project manager. Effective and efficient project management is a critical success factor for any project (Johnston 1995) and it is assumed that the necessary skills for this are in place. The process described here for benefits realisation does not prescribe a particular approach to information systems project management such as PRINCE (Bradley 1996).

6.3 Resources committed to the project

Once the project manager has been appointed the first issue to be addressed is that of project deliverables as referenced in item 3.3 of the PP. These are initially defined in terms of products. Products are then specified in terms of activities and resources required.

	Project issues
3.1	Project title
3.2	Project manager
3.3	Project deliverables—major products
3.4	Project activities—detailed tasks
3.5	Resources available
3.6	Project duration, time consumed and target completion date
3.7	Current best estimate of completion date, with rationale
3.8	Budget, actuals and cost variances-to-date
3.9	Percentage of job finished by time, cost and by specification
3.10	Forthcoming bottlenecks identified
3.11	Changes identified by formative processes
3.12	Additional funds and time available
3.13	Major risks
3.14	Major change in risk profile
3.15	Date of last and next formal review

Figure 8.17: Project Picture (PP)

However the main section of this picture is devoted to the issue of monitoring resource utilisation and item 3.6 refers to the project duration, time consumed and target completion date.

Project duration, time consumed, and target completion date are all related concepts and thus they all impact each other. The duration of the project refers to the estimated elapsed time which it is anticipated that the project will take to complete and be commissioned. When determining time consumed and target completion date organisations need to consider the concepts of elapsed months and the number of person months involved. For example the original time estimates may be 15 elapsed months requiring an input of 200 person months.

Item 3.7 specifies the current best estimate of completion date, with rationale. During the development of the initial PP this item will normally be omitted. However with subsequent iterations and updated PPs this item will be included. Issues which are addressed here are predominantly associated with problems which have arisen and have subsequently caused an alteration in the completion date of the project. The main issue which needs to be addressed here is if the project is beginning to fall behind schedule. Thus this item includes the best estimate of the completion date together with the rationale as to why this date alters from previous estimates.

6.4 Budget, actuals and cost variances-to-date

Item 3.8 concerns the reporting of the financial figures which will have been accumulated by the organisation's accounting systems for expenditure on the project.

6.5 Percentage of job finished by time, cost and by specification

Item 3.9 is an estimation of the proportion of the job left to be completed.

6.6 Forthcoming bottlenecks identified

As with item 3.4, during the development of the initial PP item 3.10 may be omitted. However during subsequent iterations forthcoming bottlenecks identified may be a critical issue. The item addresses those issues which may cause a problem in the future. For example, some of the development team may have left and thus will not be included in future project development.

The reduced number of staff may thus cause the target completion date to be unachievable and therefore there needs to be a reassessment of the completion date.

6.7 Changes identified through the formative evaluation process

As the ABR programme continues so there will be an increasing number of changes identified through this formative evaluation process. In order to control this situation it is useful to record what changes have been requested and by whom and this is done through item 3.11.

6.8 Additional funds and time available

Item 3.12 is concerned with changes that are identified and proposed through the formative evaluation process. These can only be accommodated if adequate additional funds can be made available. It is important to document if this has been the case and what the resulting new budgets and time horizons are.

6.9 Major risks

The risks that are identified in item 3.13 of the PP are very similar to those that would have been identified during the BP. However these risks are not as broad as those previously stated and are predominantly related to specific project risks. Major risks that will be identified here are to do with time, budget and quality factors.

6.10 Change in risk profile

Item 3.14 is clearly not used in preparing the initial PP. It is used in the review process and expresses, through a set of precise statements, the changes in the risks identified in item 3.10 above.

6.11 Date of last and formal review

In order to ensure that regular formative evaluation sessions are held, item 3.15 highlights when the last such meeting occurred and when the next one is scheduled to be held.

7. SUMMARY AND CONCLUSION

This chapter has addressed the development of the three pictures which are at the heart of ABR. It has explained on a step by step basis how to create each of the pictures and how the three pictures interrelate to one another. Because ABR is underpinned by the belief that sometimes not enough attention is given to the real business issues, it is suggested that the initial business picture needs to be given the most attention. It is after all from the business picture that the other two views of the information system requirements springs.

9

The Continuous Participative Evaluation Process

'Wisdom lies neither in fixity nor in change, but in the dialectic between the two'

Octavio Paz, Mexican Poet, The Times, 1989.

1. INTRODUCTION

This chapter addresses the process involved in continuous participate evaluation (CPE) and discusses the detail of how these activities are managed. This discussion assumes that the three initial pictures have been produced and that the information systems development work has begun. The post-modern approach towards information systems development implies that there is an open door attitude between the various stakeholders from all levels in the organisation and that any individual stakeholder may bring to the attention of the project manager any issue related to the project at any time. In addition to this there are, of course, regular scheduled meeting between the primary stakeholders. The open door attitude leads to what is described as continuous evidence collection.

Thus CPE implies:

1. a frequent evaluation of the information systems development;

2. a participative evaluation process;

3. a continuous focus on the business objectives of the information systems investment for the business;

4. a continuous focus on the quality of the information system, including technological quality but not dominated by technology issues;

5. an acceptance that the objectives will evolve, influenced by management, external factors, organisational needs or information systems development problems.

2. THE FORMATIVE EVALUATION PHASE

The formative evaluation phase of the CPE process illustrated in Figure 9.1 requires all the stakeholders to be able to develop views as to how the project is progressing and to be able to exchange these views in open and constructive discussion.

The first issue raised in Figure 9.1 is that of continuous evidence collection. This means that the stakeholders should remain informed on a continuous basis as to how the project is proceeding and also be familiar with any developments in the original business opportunity or problem. The stakeholders need to be prepared to think about the way the project has been specified and to produce ideas, where appropriate for improvements. It is in fact this continuous evidence collection process which will be reduced to formal reports and presented during the more formal variance report session.

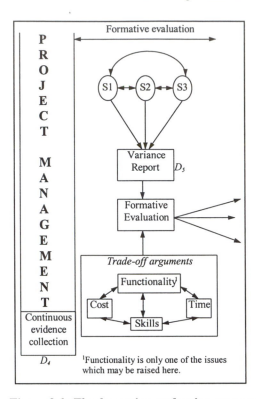

Figure 9.1: The formative evaluation process

Figure 9.1 also shows the three sets of stakeholders S1, S2 and S3, participating in the formative review. The stakeholders are joined in Figure 9.1 by bi-directional arrows which indicates inter-activity between all three groups which has been described in a previous chapter as co-evolution. This is achieved by the open discussion of their various requirements and how these may develop or change during the course of the project.

Although the stakeholders should be prepared to discuss urgent aspects of a project at short notice formal formative review sessions need to be set at regular intervals[1] for the purposes of a

---

[1] Some organisations only hold these regular meetings once a month. On shorter projects or on projects where there is a high degree of concern about its viability, review sessions may be held more frequently, perhaps once a week. Where possible

point by point review of the pictures. The exact duration of this interval will depend upon the nature and the size of the project. At these sessions variance reports will be formally considered that will indicate how the project is proceeding relative to the original plan. In addition all the stakeholders will be invited to state their current view of the project, especially if their original requirements have changed or developed.

A particularly important part of Figure 9.1 is the box which shows the trade-off arguments. This is where scope creep is handled. Scope creep may be defined as the tendency for information systems projects to expand in order to embrace a wider range of issues than originally intended. When scope creep occurs it is frequently the result of an evolution in the context. However there are occasions when scope creep has been the direct result of a greater benefit target or outcome being required. Where additional requirements arise there will certainly be the need for more time, more funds and perhaps more skills. This may be the result of a new need for more functionality in the information system or some other important change in the information system's parameters.

As scope creep is a very common occurrence and as it frequently leads to information systems' delays and cost over-runs it is essential that this issue to treated formally during the formative evaluation process. Difficult decisions frequently have to be made and these need to be debated and trade-off arguments will have to be developed.

Although ABR requires a positive attitude towards change, any suggestion of change to the project needs to be accompanied by a detailed explanation as to why this is important and how it will

---

some sort of project objective or deliverable should be associated with the regular project meetings.

improve the information system outcome. In addition an estimation of the cost, time and skill impact should be supplied.

It is at this stage that compromise may well be required. If compromises are not forthcoming then it will be necessary to appeal to higher authority. This simply means elevating the discussion to the next level up the management hierarchy in the organisation. If there is still a dispute at this level then the debate is raised one layer higher in the hierarchy and so on until consensus is reached at a more senior management level.

Although this process sounds relatively straightforward and easy to implement it is actually very difficult and it is arguably the most tricky aspect of ABR. Decisions passed down from higher levels of management without the active consent of the lower levels are frequently resented and thus not implemented in the spirit with which they were intended. This can lead to a large number of problems, especially in the implementation of information systems. Thus the use of corporate power should be the very last resort. If the co-creation and co-evolutionary attitude inherent in post-modern thinking and described in previous chapters is employed then the occurrence of confrontational incidents should be minimised. Of course it will never be possible to entirely eliminate turf wars but organisations which have a strong sense of corporate purpose tend to minimise conflicts.

3. OUTCOMES OF FORMATIVE EVALUATION

From Figure 9.2 it may be seen that there are three possible outcomes of such debates which are referred to as the way ahead, i.e. the resetting of the business, financial and project pictures, after the project has been through a formative evaluation session and thus the closing of the feedback loop.

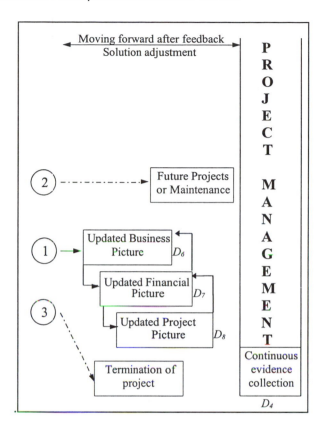

Figure 9.2: Moving forward after closing of the feedback loop

The first alternative available which is described as 1, in the three inter-linking boxes D6, D7 and D8 in Figure 9.2 above, actually occurs if any one of the following three events or sets of circumstances take place.

1. The first set of circumstances is that the project is on course and requires no changes or adjustment. In this event the initial business, financial and project pictures remain unchanged except for the fact that they are endorsed with the date of the formative review and the project continues exactly as per the initial plan.

2. The second set of circumstances is that the project requires changes, but that the changes are not material and that they can be incorporated into the project without any need for further skill, money or delays. When this occurs the business, financial and project picture are appropriately updated and the project proceeds on schedule.

3. The third set of circumstances is that the changes proposed for the project are material, but that the initiator of the suggestion to change has already arranged sufficient funds, has identified the skills required and has agreed with the eventual users that a revised delivery time is acceptable. If the time, money and skill issues are already addressed to the satisfaction of the stakeholders then all that remains is for the business, financial and project picture to be appropriately updated and the project proceeds according to the new schedule.

All three of the above scenarios simply require updates to the three pictures, which are re-written and described as D6, D7 and D8 in Figure 9.2 above, and the project proceeds.

The second alternative, which is described as 2 in Figure 9.2 above, is that the project may need to be substantially re-formed and there may not be sufficient funds, time or skills available. By this is meant that one or more of the primary stakeholders realises during the continuous evidence collection process or the formative evaluation session that the intended outcome is not really appropriate and they propose a material change to the way the original business solution is currently perceived and defined. If this is a sizeable change then frequently the only way of coping with this is to declare that the required changes will be available in a second release. In some organisations where there is no experience of second releases then the required changes will be noted and scheduled to be attended to under the title of maintenance.

The third alternative which is described as 3 in Figure 9.2 above, is that the project may have become for one or more reasons irrelevant to the organisation's business requirements. This should result in project termination.

4. RELATIVELY ROUTINE PROJECTS

In fact as a result of the formative evaluation session described some new requirements will almost invariably arise even in relatively routine projects. And as stated above where relatively minor changes to the business solution are required these can be easily handled by adjusting the initial pictures which will then be referred to as the *updated pictures*.

The updated pictures will become the documents which will be used as input to the next formative evaluation session. This produces a feedback loop which ensures that the business, financial and project pictures are not out of date or out of touch with the actual requirements. This will probably result in some scope creep but at least the extent of this will be fully documented in the updated pictures and all the stakeholders will be fully aware of its implications to both the project funding and the time required. On the other hand if more substantial alterations to the solution are required they may have to be dealt with through future projects or perhaps under the heading of future maintenance. Although it is not particularly satisfactory to use maintenance for the purposes of project enhancement it is unfortunately a fact of information systems project life.

On some occasions the proposed changes will be so large or so fundamental to the project architecture that the whole project may have to be abandoned and restarted at a different time and under a different name.

However it is the objective of an ABR programme to minimise the number of occasions that a project is abandoned or requires very substantial alterations by first devoting effort to preparing a comprehensive and sound Initial Business Picture and then focusing on the co-creation and the co-evolutionary aspects of information systems development work.

5. IMPLEMENTING AN ABR PROGRAMME

There are a number of issues which need to be considered in implementing an ABR programme and these include: Who should undertake the work? What tools are available? What cost will be incurred? and Can results be guaranteed? Although it is not possible to give precise generic answers to each of these questions some rough guidelines are provided which will be applicable in a large number of cases.

5.1 Who should undertake the work?

An ABR programme requires a team of specialists who understand the business as well as understand finance, project management and information technology and who can work closely with the stakeholders. Such a group may be created on an ad hoc basis to set the ABR programme in motion and they will then be needed from time to time to help at least with the initial formative evaluation session. As described earlier the stakeholders are likely to evolve over time and so are the other specialist members of an ABR programme team.

5.2 What tools are available?

There are a range of tools available which include subsets of project management methodologies, financial analysis packages and templates. However an ABR programme does not require a specialist software tool. It is rather a conceptual approach or framework to information systems and information development management. Benefits realisation mostly requires a change of attitude rather than the acquisition of hardware and software.

5.3 What costs will be incurred?

The costs of an ABR programme is clearly a function of the size of the project. It need not be expensive unless outside consultants are required. Even if this is the case the consultants should only be used as catalysts and therefore not a great deal of their time is essential. Whichever way an ABR programme is pursued its total cost should not exceed more than a few percent of the total cost of the project. In return for this cost an ABR programme should deliver a very much enhanced benefit stream to the organisation.

5.4 Can results be guaranteed?

Although results can never be guaranteed the probability of realising benefits are substantially enhanced by the use of an ABR programme. Even if only the first phase of the process is undertaken, that is the initial picture development phase, considerable benefit will be derived for all the stakeholders involved.

6. GETTING STARTED

At the outset it is critical to gain executive sponsorship for an idea. Thus the first step in applying ABR is the gaining of executive sponsorship for an idea. There are several issues involved in this process.

6.1 Idea or strategic generator

New ideas bombard the organisation all the time. It seems that most organisations are primarily concerned with defending themselves from this bombardment, rather than the adoption of new ideas. If there is to be coherent adoption of new ideas, then these ideas need to be verified or validated within a strategic context, and if valid, need to vie for organisational resources along with all the other valid ideas. This implies that a business case should be prepared. Traditionally, the information systems case has been a dry thing indeed; with an overt concentration on costs and benefits and with the inert assumption that the simple production of a systems output will derive the necessary benefits.

The ABR approach requires that new ideas are presented as business outcomes or improvements to business processes. Similarly the company strategy will translate into a business outcome. Thus it becomes possible to compare strategic initiatives and new ideas when the new idea occurs.

6.2 Define the business vision

By representing ideas and strategy in outcome terms, there is a focus on the process improvements needed by the business. Once proper attention is paid to the business process improvements, it becomes natural that the process improvement benefits are recognised. Underlying both the process improvement, and the benefit model, is the business *intention*. The intention provides a context against which all change is compared.

There are probably very few, if any, projects that are specified 'correctly' at the outset. The advantage of specifying an outcome space is that provided the business intention remains at the centre of the discussion, the need for absolute correctness is obviated. Outcomes do not have to be right first time; the ABR approach recognises that change will occur both in our understanding of the nature of our problem, and in the outcome space. Thus this approach leaves the door open to change.

6.3 Define a project idea in terms of outcomes

Traditionally information systems ideas have been defined in terms of systems outputs such as the types of reports required, the input screens needed to capture data, the nature of the algorithm to be used, to mention only three. ABR requires that systems or project ideas be defined at a much higher level. This means that a new idea needs, at least in the initial stages of a project, to be expressed in terms of the business value which it will deliver to the organisation. It is the potential business value which actually drives all business investment and in focusing on this aspect of an information system, ABR is simply bringing the information systems department into line with the rest of the organisation.

The first step in defining the outcome is to develop a macro model. Once there is a clear view of the higher level issues then the other aspects of the business picture may be defined. In due course the business picture will be further developed and added to until all the necessary detail is acquired for a feasibility study, which will contain the detail from the financial and project pictures which will result in executive approval for the project.

6.4 Assembling the stakeholder group

After executive approval has been gained, it becomes necessary to assemble the stakeholder group. This exercise is not trivial, because proper attention must be given to whether each member has a legitimate interest in the project, and it is imperative that political appointees be minimised.

6.4.1 Teams vs. groups

Selection of stakeholders should be based on the value that the stakeholder will bring to the project. This suggests that the stakeholder must have a legitimate interest in the project outcome: they must be affected by the project outcome or be able to affect it. They should generally represent a constituency in which they hold some sort of organisational power[2].

6.4.2 Difficulties in the selection of stakeholders

One of the more harmful practices in the selection of stakeholders is the inclusion of stakeholders because of their position in the organisation. This practice is difficult to overcome as positional power tends to also be coercive (someone can be made to comply). It is essential that every effort be made during the selection process not to select stakeholders purely because of their position, because this will involve sub-optimisation and inefficiencies later. The benefit

---

[2] The definition of power follows those types defined by Brill and Worth (1997)— coercive, formal, expert, moral referent or relationship power.

stakeholder matrix described in Chapter Eight may be useful in keeping the attention of the stakeholders. The stakeholder group will itself change through the project, and political appointments can be redressed at a later stage.

A further difficulty in the selection of stakeholders is that the organisation's most effective people are often their busiest. Conversely, people who are readily available to serve, may be ineffective. The presentation of business outcomes should be sufficiently compelling so as to free up the effective people to serve as stakeholders.

6.4.3　*The work of the stakeholder group*

During its involvement with the CPE process, the stakeholder group serves three primary functions:

1. They act as a directorship of the project. They monitor progress and change, and debate trade-offs and priorities. They assess whether change to meaning of outcome words is material to the goals. They manage change to the project goals, and assess the impact that outcomes will have on the organisation.

2. Their opinions are one of the key sources of input into the project. Thus they bring new ideas and learning to the project. They resolve input conflicts through structured negotiation within the outcome context and lexicon. They manage political activities both inside the project and within their constituency. They gain agreement on compromises that may be necessary. If a compromise solution is not reached, and a member of the stakeholder group uses his or her power to force through a solution, then the outcome is likely to be sub-optimised.

3. The stakeholder group sponsors the project at a more immediate level than the executive group. They represent the project to the rest of the organisation, and initiate the organisational changes that need to take place if the outcomes are to be achieved. The stakeholder group is also responsible for organisational learning that occurs as a result of the project, and disseminate that learning into the organisation.

7. WHO MANAGES THE CPE PROCESS?

A central issue which needs addressing when applying ABR is defining who undertakes the different activities. These activities and the parties responsible are detailed in Figure 9.3.

Activity	Idea champion	Executive	Stake-holders	Project Manager	Project Team
Outcome definition	●		•		
Executive sponsorship		●			
Stakeholder selection		●	•		
Project representation & directorship			●		
CPE process management				●	
Outputs and goals					●
Outcome attainment	•		●		
Benefit Realisation			●		

● **A high level of involvement** • **A relatively low level of involvement**

Figure 9.3: Responsibilities for activities in the ABR process

7.1 Who produces the outcome definition?

Outcome definition involves the preparation of the macro model, and then the initial business picture, the initial financial picture, and the initial project picture. Finally an outcome lexicon is prepared. This work is most probably best completed by the original idea champion, or in the case when a project is initiated by the strategy of the organisation, the key stakeholder most affected by the outcome[3]. The same individual will also probably be responsible for having the idea validated by reference to the corporate strategy etc.

Outcome models and pictures and project lexicon are continuously updated once the project has been initiated, and the primary stakeholder group takes responsibility for this task.

7.2 Who sponsors the project?

If the idea is generated by an eventual user then he or she may become the executive sponsor. If this occurs then there is the question of whether the necessary funds are available. If the idea comes from a strategy review then there will probably be a more formal structure in place to appoint an executive sponsor. Many organisations have some form of executive directorship of the information systems function, either through the aegis of the executives themselves, or through an IS Directorate Committee. This mechanism would appoint an executive sponsor.

Whatever the organisational mechanism for assigning organisational funds, people and energy to an initiative, the three

---

[3] It is in fact quite likely that one person will not have all the skills required to complete a business picture, a financial picture and a project picture. However it is important that only one person has the responsibility for producing these documents although that person may have to call upon the help of several others.

outcome pictures are presented by the executive sponsor as a business case.

7.3 Who assembles the stakeholder group?

The executive sponsor will assemble the stakeholder group, or at least appoint the primary stakeholder, and will and negotiate the necessary commitment of time and energy from the stakehold ers[4]. This is not a trivial matter and it is necessary to ensure that all the necessary stakeholders are committed before the project proceeds.

7.4 Who represents the project to the business?

The stakeholder group represents the project to the business in two ways: They are responsible to the executive for the progress of the project and for the attainment of the outcome and subsequent benefits. They also represent the project to their constituencies; if there are to be changes to business processes or work practices, the stakeholder group communicates and implements these.

---

[4] Research conducted by the authors suggests that selection of the group is easy in comparison with the task of maintaining stakeholder interest and commitment. In general, commitment is best gained when the stakeholders stand to gain from the delivery of the outcome. However it is often necessary to select stakeholders who will not be eventual users and thus who may not gain significantly from the project. Therein lies the executive challenge.

7.5 Who manages the CPE process?

The CPE process will probably be managed by the project manager. However, he or she will need continuous and substantial support and direction from the other stakeholders. The critical issue is that a participative approach is taken to the management of the project. It is important that both the project manager and the stakeholders understand the difference between participation and consultation. The project manager should expect active involvement from the stakeholders, in the same way that stakeholders can expect to have to devote significant effort to the project, rather than to be consulted periodically.

7.6 Who produces outputs and goals?

The achievement of goals and the production of project outputs is the province of the project team, which will be assembled by the organisation in its usual way in terms of the normal methodological framework used.

7.7 Who delivers the outcome?

The stakeholders bear the responsibility for attaining the outcome. They represent the project to the business, and as such need to plan, initiate, and promote the organisational and process changes which are needed to achieve the outcome. Thus, their role is significantly wider than the directorship of the project, and includes the wider organisational community which is affected by the project outcome.

7.8 Who is responsible for benefit realisation?

Benefits result from the improvements in business performance which the information system's outcome generates. Thus the business stakeholder group retains responsibility for the realisation of benefits which derive from the project.

7.9 A final word on responsibilities

While the question of reward, remuneration and recognition for participants in the above processes is beyond the scope of this book, it is important that they reflect and reinforce the expectations of individual responsibilities as suggested above.

8. SUMMARY AND CONCLUSION

The 'closing of the feed-back loop' in an ABR iteration is achieved through a formative evaluation review of progress of the information systems development project in the context of the Business, Financial and Project pictures. Because this happens at regular intervals it is viewed as continuous participative evaluation process.

The review depends on the collaboration of the three prime stakeholder groups and their representatives, who through their participation, if genuinely exercised, will have continually kept in touch with the project and collected their own 'evidence' of progress as well as having been circulated with all the relevant project management reports. They will have a view of how the project is progressing with an eye to the benefits they hope to realise, their continued relevance and the timing issues.

There are three possible outcomes of the review activity, namely, the update of the business pictures, the spawning of complementary projects to be handled separately or the termination of the project. The most likely outcome for routine projects is an update of the three ABR pictures.

Participation is the key issue for the formative evaluation review. A commitment from the stakeholders for the visioning of the project, their continued commitment to realise the benefits of their vision and a commitment to negotiation and compromise to realise agreed advantageous outcomes are essential to success. This commitment will involve taking responsibility for various aspects of the CPE process. The responsibility rests heavily with the stakeholders to achieve their business goals but executive support is needed to set up the process. A project manager takes on the responsibility for the project deliverables and achieving the actual commissioning of the information system.

10

An End Note: Some Tips, Tricks and Maybe Traps

'Whoever wishes to see the world truly, to rise in thought above the tyranny of practical desires, must learn to overcome the difference of attitude towards past and future, and to survey the whole stream of time in one comprehensive vision.'

Bertrand Russell, Mysticism and Logic, 1970.

1. INTRODUCTION

Neither organisations nor their information systems departments are working well (Wheatley 1992; Lincoln 1990; Earl 1992). In papers by Remenyi and Sherwood-Smith (1996: a,b,c), it was suggested that an active benefits realisation approach to information systems management was capable of improving the situation for information systems departments by delivering lower levels of waste, reducing cost, emphasising the achievements of outcomes and benefits, and thus ensuring that information systems deliver an appropriate return on investment.

Aspects of a management philosophy underpinned by post-modernism required for active benefit realisation as well as an approach or practical framework have been provided. However there is still a substantial amount of detail to be considered regarding how to actually implement the active benefits realisation approach. It should be immediately stated that the application of ABR is an art and not a science. Although not quite so cautious the authors are reminded of Pascale's (1993) comment when he proclaimed:

> '... we don't know how to transform organisations. Notwithstanding all the talk and money spent it's just a hit-or-miss proposition.'

The implementation of ABR needs considerable care and attention based on a contingent approach which will allow ABR plans to be flexible and responsive to the organisation's changing requirements. In effect ABR itself needs to be implemented through an ABR approach.

In a sense ABR is both new[1] and subtle, requiring a shift in the way the work of the information systems function is thought about and how the work is actually done. Thus the difficulty in promoting ABR within the organisation is twofold—its newness begets resistance (Brill & Worth, 1997), and its subtlety can sometimes contribute to arming its detractors with coarse but irrelevant disavowals.

---

[1] As mentioned in Chapter One, much of the thinking underpinning active benefit realisation, especially those aspects of the approach related to formative evaluation is not really new, at least in the academic sense. However the operationalisation of active benefit realisation is quite new to most members of the information systems community. This discussion is reminiscent of the age old debate between the followers of Heraclitus who argued that everything is new i.e. 'You could not step twice into the same rivers; for other waters are ever flowing on to you', and the followers of Parmenides, who said that 'There is nothing new under the Sun'.

2. THE CRITICAL ISSUES TO MANAGE IN THE CPE PROCESS

This chapter discusses a number of issues which need to be borne in mind if ABR is to be successfully implemented. These issues are mostly related to the problems associated with the introduction of any material change programme in an organisation. The issues are simplicity, the time frame issue, project progress and the co-evolution issue, progress reports, and the contingency issue.

2.1 Simplicity

Simplicity needs to drive the process and each of the words in CPE dictates why the process needs to be simple. Because continuous referral to the outcome context is necessary, simple pictures of the business, financial and project dimensions are used, as it is substantially easier to refer often to a picture, table, list or graph, than it is to refer to a specification document. Participation implies a group process. Given that change is *expected* to occur, and that the initial pictures will be updated, the interaction between group members and change needs to be simplified and ordered. Finally, 'evaluation' suggests that gaps between the projected plan and the new plan need to be identified, assessed and managed. Thus a simple method for identifying the gaps, evaluating their impact, and managing any change that is necessary is fundamental to ABR.

However, there is a danger of oversimplifying the underlying complexities of an information systems development project and clearly this needs to be avoided. Simple pictures, models or representations need to be seen as 'cues' to an ongoing organisational dialogue. Thus the aim of simplification is to promote an incisive discussion where the most complex of issues may be handled.

2.2 The time frame issue

Time is a prime determinant of information systems project success. According to Reinertson (1983, p 35):

> '... products that came out six months late but on budget generated about 33 percent less profits over a five-year span than they would have if they had come out on schedule. On the other hand, products that came out on schedule and 50 percent over budget showed a shortfall of only 4 percent in profits for the same time span.'

As corporations have successively cut costs and reduced overheads 'down to the bone' over the last fifteen years, time represents one of the last major sources of competitive leverage (Stalk and Hout 1990; Pritchett 1994; Waterman 1994; Hamel and Prahalad 1994).

Thus, in general, the business time-cycle is under pressure, and any improvement to the time efficiency of the organisation that can be made by the information systems development process will have a direct impact on the competitiveness of the organisation. Furthermore the ability of the project to accommodate change is directly dependent on a short goal cycle-time. As is expressed by Leiven (1995, p 111):

> 'Flexibility and speed belong together. With low speed you cannot be flexible.'

Furthermore the chance of information systems' project success diminishes if goals are set beyond a three to four month horizon. As stated by Wick and León (1993, p 56):

> 'We found that goals that take 4 months to accomplish
> work best. If the time required is shorter, that's fine. If
> your goal will take longer, then break it into smaller
> pieces and select a milestone along the way that you
> can attain in 4 months.'

And Hamel and Prahalad (1994, p 156) believe that competitive
advantage is enhanced by the setting of so-called 'unreasonable',
as short a time as possible, goals:

> 'We believe that companies like NEC, Charles
> Schwab, CNN, Sony, Glaxo, Canon, and Honda were
> united by the unreasonableness of their ambitions and
> the creativity exhibited in getting the most from the
> least, than they were by a common cultural or
> institutional heritage.'

Thus it can be seen that choosing a shorter goal setting time-
frame within the larger outcome context matches more closely
with business cycles, allows for a more flexible response to
change and challenges staff.

Finally, control is improved as shorter time-frames allow for
more immediate performance monitoring and management.
Thus problems and mistakes do not remain in hiding for long.

2.3 The project progress and the co-evolution issue

The issue concerning the management of on-going progress in
an ABR project revolves around how progress is measured and
maintained in a changing or co-evolving environment without
the loss of control and discipline, and the opportunity for
making facetious excuses that this inevitably presents.

The progress of an ABR project is monitored by means of the
CPE process. Goals are set within the context of the outcome. It

is suggested that goals are set within a three month horizon and standard project management work breakdown techniques are used i.e. milestone plans, critical path networks, etc. (Turner 1993). As may be seen from the previous discussion the CPE approach is, essentially, to manage exceptions both at the conceptual and detail level to whatever plans are set in place.

2.4 Progress reports

To manage exceptions it is necessary to identify changes to the outcome definition, to the project lexicon or to the goals themselves. A visual representation of these factors assists in the identification of exceptions and it is suggested that a dashboard approach could be used. The dashboard approach is frequently discussed in terms of the balanced scorecard ideas of Kaplan and Norton (1992). They have described a 'balanced scorecard' approach as:

> 'The balanced scorecard is like the dials in an airplane cockpit: it gives managers complex information at a glance.'

A visual representation of the project objectives eases the understanding of complex issues, and acts as an invitation or cue to discuss and negotiate. The authors propose that a dashboard representation, which identifies the key outcomes, concepts and which allows for identification of change is appropriate to projects managed through the ABR framework.

A sample dashboard report outline for one outcome parameter is shown in Figure 10.1.

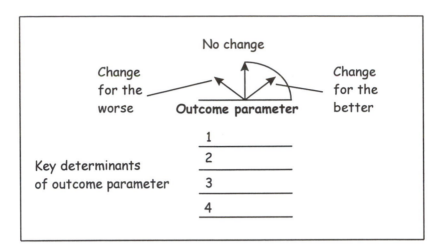

Figure 10.1: Elements of the dashboard approach

When stakeholders identify a change to an outcome parameter, they signify this change by updating the dashboard. As has been proposed, this visual notification cues the dialogue which now centres on the impact that this change will have on the outcome pictures, on the project lexicon and on the individual goals. This is at the heart of the formative evaluation process

Measurement of progress against individual goals occurs in the normal way, but when goals change, or the outcome definition changes, then the measurement of progress is more difficult. The tale is told of the leader who climbs to the top of a tall tree in a forest through which a new road is being built. When the leader calls down to the project manager: 'Hey, we're in the wrong forest!', the manager calls back: 'Yes, but we're making good progress!' This tale reflects the conundrum faced by managers when they recognise that there has been a change to the goal-posts: Do they continue on the established route, or do they accommodate the change? If the need to change is recognised and responded to then the question arises, is accommodating constant change to be seen as progress?

ABR provides the mechanism for coping with these circumstances if not for answering the deeper philosophical questions.

2.5 The contingency issue

As ABR recognises the contingent nature of all business plans and especially the high probability that information systems requirements may change, even during the development cycle, the issue of change is never far from the central concerns.

When the need for changes is identified it is then necessary to determine if there is sufficient slack in the project to be able to accommodate these requirements without having to change the time scale or add new resources.

If the changes are relatively minor then it will usually be possible to cope with them within the original project. In such a case the original business pictures are updated and the project proceeds.

However if the proposed changes are substantial it may be necessary to find additional resources and to negotiate a new delivery schedule. It is necessary for the proposer of the changes to find the additional funds and to be able to convince the eventual user to accommodate the inevitable delay in delivery. This is often a question of negotiation. Here the pictures will also be updated and the work on the new version of the project will continue. A problem arises when there are no additional resources available. In such a case it may be necessary to trade-off some currently established goals and commitments for new ones. This is done through a process of prioritisation and negotiation and frequently presents major problems and major changes for the stakeholders. In some cases the required changes will only be accommodated by delaying some goals and including them in a later project or even under the heading of maintenance.

If the proposed changes are substantial then it may be necessary to admit that the previous work will not satisfy the new circumstances and that the most effective solution is to close or terminate the project. Project termination is always a very painful event and can only be ameliorated by the knowledge that it is always less expensive to discontinue a mistake than to carry on in the false belief that somehow it will come right. In such a case some of the work already completed might be applicable to the new situation.

3. SUMMARY AND CONCLUSION

The information systems departments of many organisations are not working well especially with regard to their ability to deliver high quality information systems, on time and within budget.

Many different solutions have been proposed which are sometimes referred to as silver bullets, but, in general these have not produced material results. What is required to improve the performance of information systems development professionals is a much more fundamental re-think of their approach based on the ideas underpinning post-modernism.

ABR is not a silver bullet. ABR is not a quick fix. ABR is not a detailed methodology. ABR is ultimately a post-modern mind-set, or way of thinking, which facilitates the development of insight and understanding (Hanson 1996) of how information systems deliver outcomes, which in turn may be used to facilitate business improvements and thus deliver real benefit streams for the organisation.

In the last years of the twentieth century organisations are having to come to terms with the need for change in a number of different areas and the concepts inherent in post-modernism are a useful framework with which to think through these issues. Perhaps the most important reason why the ideas behind ABR are not yet being extensively practised is that, at the heart of ABR is the admission that change is a natural part of the organisation's life. In turn this could mean for many senior managers that all forecasts, estimates and plans have to be, by their very nature, contingent. This realisation is unsettling to managers who are products of a deterministic school of management philosophy.

However, it is not sufficient to explain the fear of change. An admission of the ubiquitous and inevitable nature of change means that the organisational and management philosophy driving organisations, especially business firms, is vulnerable to reassessment and change. Admitting the need for change means that all sorts of fundamental principles need to be questioned. Perhaps very quickly someone in the organisation will state 'Maybe, Adam Smith was wrong and business[2] is not about the maximisation of profit'. If that assumption is removed then the whole fabric of capitalism may have to be reassessed. And perhaps this should happen. Keynes (1953) himself questioned capitalism when he said:

> 'The decadent international but individualistic capitalism in the hands of which we found ourselves after the war is not a success. It is not intelligent. It is not beautiful. It is not just. It is not virtuous. And it doesn't deliver the goods.'

---

[2] It is not at all inconceivable that one day economics will be rewritten in which the main objective of business will be to produce a flow of goods and services in order to have a healthy and prosperous society, both at the national and the international level.

Perhaps this reflects the depth of the crisis in current business and management thinking. And after all Keynes (1953) did point out that:

> 'It is ideas, not vested interests, which are dangerous for good or evil.'

The second important reason why the ideas behind ABR are potentially controversial is that they clearly require a participative approach from management. As illustrated by the quotation from Konosuke Matsushita (1982) mentioned in Chapter Two, traditional management does not regard participation as a desirable phenomenon. It is not only the Japanese who see this problem in the way that organisations operate in the West. Hanson (1996) points out:

> '... structures based on command and control thinking and extrinsic reward programs designed to steer and control the human resource making us dependent on the system and separate us from our work and each other.'

In effect there is a major disconnect between people and their work especially at the non-executive level. There is frequently a huge disconnect between executives and directors and the office and factory workers who often perceive the former as remote and privileged. It is not clear that Western managers want to do much about this situation.

The third reason is the apparent loss of control and power which top and senior management could experience as a result of ABR. Participation involves a dissemination of control and power. The recognition of the inevitability of goal-post changing means that top and senior managers are not as much in control as they might wish. It is suggested that the amount of control which managers have of a business situation is almost certainly less than they would normally believe. In fact control is frequently an illusion. And denying the existence of continuous change is not a solution to the problem and denial is certainly not a form of control. Nonetheless control remains a major business issue in many organisations. Keidel (1995) clearly identified this when he wrote:

> 'The overwhelming tendency for management is to be obsessed with control.'

However control has to be paid for with a price that often reduces flexibility and creativity. The lack of responsiveness that results has led to corporate collapse. What is needed at the end of the twentieth century is a strong focus on creativity which is well expressed by Kao (1996) as follows:

> 'This is the age of creativity because there's been a change of regime in the marketplace. The customer is boss now—discerning, demanding, and no more loyal than he or she has to be. The new boss has only one question: So what are you going to do for me tomorrow? Only creativity can give the answer.'

Although ABR on its own will not solve all these problems it represents a major step in a direction which challenges management to rethink their old views and to come up with better solutions.

Specifically ABR offers a framework in which managers are able to be creative and flexible. Although this flexibility will inevitably be managed in terms of the ABR framework the spirit of Edison's (1995) comment:

> 'There aren't any rules here, we are trying to get something done.'

needs to be borne in mind as all the concepts and procedures of ABR have not yet been set in concrete.

In the final analysis the power of ABR is that it proposes the creation of a new mind-set which recognises the inevitability of change and proposes an approach which places a high value on flexibility and creativity.

ABR is a framework which if correctly implemented will produce much better results for the information systems developer and will eventually lead to achieving the maximum value for the organisation's investment in information systems.

Of course, the work in developing ABR is not complete and is unlikely ever to be so. In the words of Checkland (1986) writing about systems thinking:

> 'Obviously the work is not finished, and can never be finished. There are no absolute positions to be reached in the attempt by men to understand the world in which they find themselves: new experience may in the future refute present conjectures. So the work itself must be regarded as an on-going system of a particular kind: A learning system which will continue to develop ideas, to test them out in practice, and to learn from the experience gained.'

The study of ABR will be no less demanding.

References

Adair J, *Management Decision Making*, Gower Publishing Company Ltd., Aldershot, p 19, 1985.

Adelman C, 'Anything goes: evaluation and relativism', *Evaluation*, Vol. 2, No 3, p 291–305, Sage Publications, London, July, 1996.

Akkermans H, 'Developing a logistic strategy through participative business modelling', *International Journal of Operations and Production Management*, pp 100–112, Vol. 15, Issue 11, 1995.

Albrecht K, *The Northbound Train*, AMACOM, New York, 1994.

Allingham P, and O'Connor M, 'MIS Success: Why does it vary among users?', *Journal of Information Technology*, Vol. 7, pp 160–168, 1992.

American Heritage Dictionary of the English Language, Third Edition, Houghton Mifflin Company. From the electronic version licensed from InfoSoft International, Inc. 1992.

Argyris C, and Schon D, *Organizational Learning: A Theory of Action Perspective*, Addison-Wesley, Reading, MA, 1978.

Attewell P, *Information Technology and the Productivity Paradox*, Mimeograph, City University of New York, 1993.

Banker R, and Kemerer C F, Research undertaken on *'Performance Evaluation Metrics For Information Systems Development: A Principal-Agent Model'*, October, 1991.

Beam K, Ed., Software Engineering Productivity and Quality, *IS Analyser*, Vol. 32, No 2, 1994.

Bergout E, Klompe R and de Vries M, 'Towards enhancing investment evaluation methods with behavioural theory', *Proeceedings of the Third European Conference on The Evaluation of Information Technology*, TechTrans, Reading, 1996.

Berny J, and Townsend P, 'Macrosimulation of project risks a practical way forward', *The International Journal of Project Management*, Volume 11, Number 4, November, 1993.

Bjørn-Anderson A, (1986) cited by Willcocks L, *Unpublished Chairman's Introduction to a Conference on Managing IT Investment*, conducted by Business Intelligence, London, 20 May 1991.

Blanton J E, Watson H J, and Moody J, 'Toward a better understanding of information technology organisation: A comparative case study', *MIS Quarterly*, pp 531–555, December, 1992.

Boyton A C, and Zmud R W, 'Information technology planning in the 1990s: Directions for practice and research', *MIS Quarterly*, pp 59–71, March, 1987.

Bradley K, *Prince: A Practical Handbook*, Butterworth-Heinemann, Oxford, UK, 1996.

Brigham E F, and Gapenski L C, *Financial Management, Theory and Practice* (Second edition), The Drydon Press, Fort Worth, TX, 1994.

Brill P, and Worth R, *The Four Levers of Corporate Change*, AMACOM, New York, 1997

Brunner I, and Guzman A, 'Participatory evaluation: A tool to assess projects and empower people', in *International Innovations in Evaluation Methodology: New Directions for Evaluation Methodology*, edited by Conner R F, and Hendricks M, Jossey-Bass, San Francisco, CA, 1989.

Bruns (jnr) W J, and McFarlan F W, 'Information technology puts power in control systems', *Harvard Business Review*, Sept/Oct, 1987.

Brynjolfsson E, 'The productivity paradox of information technology', *Communications of the ACM*, Vol. 36, No. 12, pp 67–77, December, 1993.

Business Week, 'Computer industry in trouble', December, 1992.

Butler M, cited in Lincoln T, *Managing Information Systems for Profit*, John Wiley and Sons, Chichester, 1990.

Cash J I, and Konsynski B R, 'IS redraws competitive boundaries', *Harvard Business Review*, March–April, 1995.

Checkland P, *Systems Thinking, Systems Practice*, John Wiley and Sons, UK, 1986.

Chelimsky E, 'Old patterns and new directions in program evaluation', *American Society of Public Administration*, pp 1–35, 1985.

Churchman C W, *The Design of Inquiring Systems*, Basic Books Inc, New York, 1971.

Correia C, *et al. Financial Management*, Second edition, Juta & Co., Ltd, Cape Town, 1989.

Currie W, 'The art of justifying new technology to top management', *Omega*, No 17, 5 pp 409–418, 1989.

Daniels N C, *Information Technology: The Management Challenge*, Addison-Wesley Publishers Ltd., 1994.

Davenport T, *Process Innovation: Reengineering Work through Information Technology*, Harvard Business School Press, 1993.

Drury C, *Management and Cost Accounting* (Third edition), Chapman and Hall, London, 1995.

Dumas P J, *Management Information System: A Dialectic Theory and the Evaluation Issue*, Ph.D. Thesis, the University of Texas at Austin, 1978.

Earl M, 'Putting IT in its place: a polemic for the nineties', *Journal of Information systems*, September, 1992.

Economist, 'Too many computers spoil the broth', p 30, 24 August, 1991.

Edison T, attributed by Johnson M, in *Managing in the Next Millennium*, p 117, Butterworth–Heinemann, Oxford, 1995.

Farbey B, Land F, and Targett D, 'System method context: A contribution towards the development of guidelines for choosing a method of evaluating I/S investments', *Proceedings of the Second European Conference on Information Technology Investment Evaluation*, Henley Management College, 11–12 July, 1995.

Finne H, Levin M, and Nilssen T, 'Trailing research: A model for useful program evaluation', *Evaluation*, Vol. 1, No 1, July 1995, Sage Publications, London, UK.

Foster R, *Innovation The Attacker's Advantage*, Summit Books, New York, 1986.

Gellerman S W, 'In organisations, as in architecture, form follows function', *Organisation Dynamics*, Winter 1990.

Gonin R, and Money A H, *Nonlinear L_p Norm Estimation*, Marcel Dekker, 1989.

Gould S J, *The Mismeasure of Man*, p 27, Penguin Books, London, 1992.

Grindley K, *Managing IT At Board Level*, Pitman Publishing, London, 1991.

Guba E G, and Lincoln Y S, *Fourth Generation Evaluation*, Sage, London, 1989.

Habermas J, *Postmetaphysical Thinking Philosophical Essays*, p 3, translated by Hohengarten, The MIT Press, Cambridge MA, 1993.

Hamel G, and Prahalad C K, *Competing for the Future*, Harvard Business School Press, Boston, MA, 1994.

Handy C, *The Age of Unreason*, Arrow Books, London, p 71, 1989.

Hanson D, *A Place to Shine*, Butterworth–Heinemann, Boston, MA,1996.

Hansen G S, and Wernerfelt B, 'Determinants of Firm Performance: The relative importance of economic and organisational factors', *Strategic Management Journal*, Vol. 10, pp 553–567, 1989.

Heafield A, *The Evaluation of Information Systems Success*, Unpublished research dissertation, Department of Information Systems, University of the Witwatersrand, South Africa, 1995.

Henderson J C, and Treacy M E, 'Managing end-user computing for competitive advantage', *Sloan Management Review*, Winter, 1986.

Hertz D, 'Risk analysis and capital investment appraisal', *Harvard Business Review*, Vol 46, p 96, Jan–Feb 1968.

Hewett T T, 'The role of iterative evaluation in designing systems usability', *Proceedings of 2nd. BCS HCI Specialist Group Conference, People and Computers: Designing for Usability*. Harrison, M. D. and Monk. (Eds.), York, 1986.

Heygate R, *The McKinsey Quarterly*, pp 79–86, Number 2, 1993.

Hirschheim R, and Smithson S, 'A critical analysis of information systems evaluation', in *IS Assessment: Issues and Challenges*, edited by Bjørn-Andersen N, and Davis G, North Holland, Amsterdam, 1988.

Hitt L, and Brynjolfsson E, 'The three faces of IT value: theory and evidence', *Proceedings of the Fifteenth International Conference on Information Systems*, Vancouver, British Columbia, Canada, December 14–17, 1994.

Hogbin G, and Thomas D, *Investing in Information Technology Managing the Decision Making Process*, McGraw-Hill Book Company, Maidenhead, 1994.

Hopwood A G, 'Evaluating the real benefits', in *New Office Technology, Human and Organisational Aspect*, edited by Otway H J, and Peltu M, Pinter Ltd., London, 1983.

House E R, *Professional Evaluation: Social Impact and Political Consequences*, Sage Publications Inc., Beverly Hills, CA, 1993.

Johnson N L, and Kotz S, *Distributions in Statistics: Continuous Univariate Distributions*, Volumes 1 and 2, Houghton Mifflin, Boston, MA,1970.

Johnston A, *A Hacker's Guide to Project Management*, Butterworth–Heinemann, Oxford, 1995.

Johnston H R, and Carrico S R, 'Developing capabilities to use information strategically', *MIS Quarterly*, March, 1988.

Jung C G, *Memories, Dreams, Reflections*, p 17, Fontana Press, London, 1995

Kao J, *Jamming The Art & Discipline of Business Creativity*, p 14, HarperCollins, London, 1996

Kaplan R S, and Norton D P, 'The balanced scorecard; measures that drive performance', *Harvard Business Review*, Vol. 70, No. 1, 1992.

Karlin S, *11th R.A. Fisher Memorial Lecture*, Royal Society, London, April 20, 1983.

Keen P, 'Computer based decision aids: the evaluation problem', *Sloan Management Review*, 16(3), pp 17–29, 1975.

Keen P, *Shaping the Future Business Design Through Information Technology*, Harvard Business School Press, Boston, MA, p142, 1991.

Keidel R W, *Seeing Organizational Patterns; A New Theory and Language of Organizational Design*, Berret Koehler, San Francisco, CA, 1995.

Kettinger W J, and Lee C C, 'Perceived service quality and user satisfaction with the information services function', *Decision Sciences*, Vol. 25, No. 5/6, pp 737–765, 1995.

Keynes J M, *The General Theory of Employment, Interest and Money*, (first published in 1936), Harcourt Brace Jovanich, Orlando, FL, 1953.

Koella J, 'On the use of mathematical models of malaria transmission', *Acta*, 49, p 2, 1991.

Konosuke Matsushita (1982) cited in Pascale, R, *Managing on the Edge*, Penguin Books, London, 1990.

Krugman P, *The Age of Diminished Expectations*, MIT Press, Cambridge, MA, 1992.

Kumar K, 'Post implementation evaluation of computer based information systems: Current practices', *Communications of the ACM*, Vol. 33, No.2, pp 203–212, February, 1990.

Lederer A L, and Sethi P, 'Meeting the challenges of information systems planning', *Long Range Planning*, Vol. 25, No 2, pp 69–80, 1992.

Legge K, *Evaluating Planned Organisational Change*, Academic Press, London, 1984.

Leiven T, cited in Johnson M, *Managing in the Next Millennium*, Butterworth–Heinemann, Oxford, 1995.

Lester S, and Willcocks L, 'How do organisations evaluate and control information systems investments? Recent UK Survey evidence', Adapted from a study by the same authors: *Evaluation and Control of IS Investments: Recent UK Survey Evidence*, Oxford Institute of Information Management, 1993.

Lincoln T, *Managing Information Systems for Profit*, John Wiley and Sons, Chichester,1990.

Lodge L, 'A user-led model of systems development', in *Participation in Systems Development*, edited by Knight K, Kogan Page and Unicom, London, 1989.

Love A, 'Internal evaluation: Building organisations from within', *Applied Social Research Methods Series*, Vol. 24, SAGE Publications, Newbury Park, CA, 1991.

Maynard Smith J, *Models in Ecology*, p 1 Cambridge University Press, Cambridge, 1975.

McFarlan F W, 'Information technology changes the way you compete', *Harvard Business Review*, May– June, 1984.

McFarlan F W, *A video produced on the subject of information management*, Harvard Business School, 1990.

McKeen J, and Smith H, *Management Challenges in IS, Successful Strategies and Appropriate Actions*, John Wiley and Son, Chichester, 1996.

Medawar P, *The Limits of Science*, p 6, Oxford University Press, Oxford, 1986.

Morley C, 'Information systems development and user participation: A contingency approach', in *Human, Organizational and Social Dimensions of IS Development*, edited by Avison D, Kendall J E, and DeGross J I, pp 127–142, North Holland, Amsterdam, 1993.

Mumford E, *Designing Human Systems,* Manchester Business School, Manchester, 1983.

Mumford E, and Henshall D A, *A Participative Approach to Computer Systems Design*, Associated Business Press, London, 1979.

Niederman F, Brancheau J C, and Wetherbe J C, 'Information systems management issues for the 1990s', *MIS Quarterly*, Vol. 15, No. 4, pp 475–500, 1991.

Parasuraman A, Zeithaml V A, and Berry L L, 'SERVQUAL: A multiple-item scale for measuring consumer perceptions of service quality', *Journal of Retailing*, Vol. 64, No. 1, pp 12–40, Spring, 1988.

Pascale R, *Managing on the Edge*, Penguin Books, London, 1990.

Pascale R, 'Surviving success, the new challenge for change leaders', *Insights Quarterly*, CSC Index, Summer, 1993.

Patton M Q, *Qualitative Evaluation Methods*, Sage Publications Inc, Beverley Hills, CA, 1980.

Patton M Q, *Utilization Focused Evaluation*, Sage Publications Inc, Beverley Hills, CA, 1986.

Peters T, *Thriving on Chaos*, Macmillan Publishers, New York, NY,1987.

Porter M E, *Competitive Strategy Techniques for Analysing Industries and Competitors*, The Free Press, New York, NY, 1985.

Premkumar G, and King W R, 'Organisational characteristics and information systems planning: An empirical study', *Information Systems Research*, Vol. 5, No. 2, pp 75 – 109, June, 1994.

Pritchett P, *New Work Habits for a Radically Changing World*, Pritchett & Assoc, Dallas, TX, p 10, 1994.

Proctor T, 'Business modelling on a personal computer', *Management Decision*, pp 38–43, Vol. 33, Issue 9, 1995.

Pyburn P J, 'Redefining the role of IT', *Business Quarterly*, Vol. 55, No. 3, 1991.

Raho L, Belohav J, and Fielder K, 'Assimilating new technology into an organisation' *An Assessment of McFarlan and McKinneys Model*, 1987.

Rebien C C, 'Participatory evaluation of development assistance', *Evaluation*, Vol. 2, No. 2, pp 151–171, Sage Publications, London, March, 1996.

Reinertson D G, *Whodunit? The Search for the New-Product Killers*, McKinsey & Co, 1983.

Remenyi D, *Increase Profits with Strategic Information Systems,* NCC, Manchester, 1988.

Remenyi D, *Strategic Information Systems, Development and Implementation Case Studies,* NCC–Blackwell, Oxford, 1990.

Remenyi D, Money A, and Twite A, *The Effective Measurement and Management of IT Costs and Benefits*, Butterworth-Heinemann, Oxford, 1995.

Remenyi D, and Sherwood-Smith M, 'Active benefits realisation using a formative evaluation approach', *Working paper, Department of Information Systems*, University of the Witwatersrand, Johannesburg, 1996a.

Remenyi D, and Sherwood-Smith M, 'An active benefits realisation approach to information systems project management', *Working paper, Department of Information Systems,* University of the Witwatersrand, Johannesburg, 1996b.

Remenyi D, and Sherwood-Smith M, 'Another look at evaluation to achieve maximum value from information systems', *Working paper, Department of Information Systems,* University of the Witwatersrand, Johannesburg, 1996c.

Sankar Y, 'Implementing information technology: A managerial audit for planning change', *Journal of Systems Management,* November, 1991.

Schaefer G, (Editor), *Functional Analysis of Office Requirements: A Multi-Perspective Approach,* John Wiley and Sons, Chichester, 1988.

Schall L D, and Haley C W, *Introduction to Financial Management* (Sixth edition), McGraw–Hill Book Co., Singapore, 1991.

Scriven M, 'The Methodology of Evaluation', in *Perspectives of Curriculum Evaluation,* edited by Tyler R W, Gagne R M, and Scriven M, Rand McNally, Chicago. IL, 1967.

Scriven M S, 'The science of valuing', in *Foundations of Program Evaluation: Theories and Practice,* by Shadish W R, *et al.,* Sage, Newbury Park, CA, 1991a.

Scriven M S, *Evaluation thesaurus,* 4th Edition, Sage, Newbury Park, CA, 1991b

Selig F F, 'Managing information technology in the Nineties', *Information and Management,* 1991.

Senge P, *The Fifth Discipline The Art and Practice of the Learning Organisation,* Random House, Sydney, Australia, 1992.

Serafeimidis V, and Smithson S, 'The management of change for a rigorous appraisal of IT investment: The case of a UK insurance organisation', *Proceedings of the Third European Conference on Information Systems*, pp 221–233, June 1–3, Athens, 1995.

Shadish W R, Cook T D, and Leviton L C, *Foundations of Program Evaluation: Theories of Practice,* Sage Publications, Newbury Park, CA, 1991.

Sherman S, Personal notes from a lecture given by Stratford Sherman on 26th February 1994 in Johannesburg. Sherman is a staff writer for *Fortune* magazine, New York and has written the book: '2020 Vision'.

Shorter Oxford English Dictionary, revised and edited by C T Onions, Oxford, 1983.

Silk, D J, Managing IS benefits for the 1990s, *Journal of Information Technology*, Vol. 5, 1990.

Stalk G, and Hout T, *Competing Against Time*, The Free Press, New York, 1990.

Strassman P A, *The Business Value of Computers,* The Information Economics Press, 1990.

Symons V, 'A review of information systems evaluation: Content, context and process', *European Journal of Information Systems*, No. 1, 3 pp 205–212, 1991.

Symons V, 'Evaluation of information systems investment: towards multiple perspectives', in *Information Management The Evaluation of Information Systems Investment*, Edited by Willcocks L, Chapman and Hall, London, 1994.

Synnott W, *The Information Weapon,* John Wiley and Sons, Chichester, 1987.

Thompson J D, *Organisation in Action,* McGraw–Hill, New York, 1967.

Townsend R, *Further Up the Organization,* Knopf, New York, 1984.

Treacy M, and Wiersema F, 'Customer intimacy and other value disciplines', *Harvard Business Review,* pp 84–93, Jan–Feb, 1993.

Turner R, *The Handbook of Project Based Management,* McGraw–Hill, Maidenhead, 1993.

Turner J R, *The Commercial Project Manager,* McGraw–Hill, Maidenhead, 1995.

Walsham G, *Interpreting Information Systems in Organisations,* John Wiley and Sons, Chichester, 1993.

Ward J, Taylor P, and Bond P, 'Evaluation and realisation of IS/IT benefits: an empirical study of current practices', *European Journal of Information Systems,* No. 4, pp 214–225, 1996.

Waterman R, *The Frontiers of Excellence,* Nicholas Brealey Publishing, London, 1994.

Wheatley M J, *Leadership and the New Science,* Berret Koehler, San Francisco, CA, 1992

Wiersema F, *Customer Intimacy,* p 38, Knowledge Exchange, Santa Monica, CA, 1996.

Willcocks L *Unpublished Chairman's Introduction to a Conference on Managing IT Investment*, conducted by Business Intelligence, London, 20 May, 1991.

Willcocks L, *Information Management   The evaluation of information systems investment*, Chapman & Hall, London, 1994.

Wilson D, 'Assessing the impact of information technology on organisational performance', in *Strategic Information Technology Management*, edited by Banker R, Kauffman P, and Maymood M A, Ideas Group, Harrisburg, Pennsylvania, 1993.

Winograd T, and Flores F, *Understanding Computers and Cognition: A New Foundation for Design*, Ablex Corporation, Norwood, NJ, 1987.

Wiseman C, *Strategy and Computers   Information Systems as Competitive Weapons*, DowJones Irwin, London, 1985.

Zelm M, Vernadat F, and Kosanke K, 'The CIMOSA business modelling process', *Computers in Industry*, pp 123–142, Vol. 26, Issue 2, October, 1995.

Zuboff S, *In the Age of the Smart Machine: The Future of Work and Power*, Basic Books, New York, 1988.

List of Acronyms

ABR	Active Benefit Realisation
BRP	Benefit Realisation Programme
CBA	Cost Benefit Analysis
CPE	Continuous Participative Evaluation
CSF	Critical Success Factors
IBP	Initial Business Picture
IFP	Initial Financial Picture
IPP	Initial Project Picture
KPI	Key Performance Indicators
MGPS	Moving Goal-Post Syndrome
NPV	Net Present Value
ROI	Return On Investment
SDLC	Software Development Life Cycle
SIS	Strategic Information System

Glossary of Terms

Active benefit realisation (ABR): The active benefit realisation process is a non-traditional approach to information system conceptualisation and development. ABR may also be used to continually assess and manage information systems already in use. Through a high degree of openness or *glasnost*, which involves information systems professionals playing a co-evolutionary role, together with line managers and users, as well as financial staff, more effective information systems may be developed. This means that information systems no longer need to be tied into single purpose-built developments created by technicians, but can be the product of co-creation and co-evolutionary collaboration involving all the principal stakeholders. Central to this collaboration is the inclusion of a feedback loop, based on evaluation which will allow appropriate interventions to take place during information systems development and management, leading to a much higher degree of information systems success. The ABR process is based on a contingency philosophy based on post-modern management thinking to the specification of the precise tasks and activities of a particular information systems development project. By contingency philosophy is meant that the actual information system outcomes as well as the development activities, tasks and participating roles of the stakeholders are not cast in concrete and unchanging, but are recognised as dynamic throughout the duration of the project. Fundamental to the ABR approach is that the principal stakeholders of the information system are identified at the onset and that they accept and agree their continuous involvement.

Approach: In the context of this book an approach is a way of dealing with and accomplishing satisfactory results with information systems development.

Benefit: A term used to indicate an advantage, profit or gain attained by an individual or organisation. A benefit is normally traded-off against a cost of some sort.

Benefit realisation programme (BRP): is a series of activities and tasks which need to be undertaken if an information system project is to produce an improvement in effectiveness or efficiency, or deliver some other advantages originally believed possible. Active Benefit Realisation is realised through a benefit realisation programme.

Business futuring: A means by which information systems professionals or other business professionals concentrate on defining proposed business outcomes, identify changes in goals as the stakeholders become clearer on the outcome conditions and track progress towards these outcomes. This involves a vision of the required future and being able to manage the steps necessary to achieve this future. Inevitably this will involve identifying the gaps between the present situation and the desired future outcome and managing the closing of this gap.

Business objectives: Those objectives a business organisation wishes to achieve. In the context of this book, the organisational changes and improvements that are to be achieved in order to enhance the business performance as a result of the information system's development and commissioning.

Business value: Something of worth to the organisation. Business value refers to how much the information system contributes to the overall worth of the business. This does not simply refer to short term cost improvements but to a full range of issues including both hard and soft benefits.

Business vision: The business vision is that which the management want to achieve with the enterprise in the future. A business vision usually refers to the medium to long term. It is often expressed in terms of a series of specific objectives as well as general values.

Capital investment: Funds committed to long term assets within the firm such as land and building, plant and equipment or computer hardware. In some cases computer software is even regarded as a capital investment.

Co-creation: A co-creation approach means that all the stakeholders' interests are considered in deciding how to originally specify the proposed information system at the outset.

Co-evolutionary: A co-evolutionary approach means that all the stakeholders' interests are considered in deciding how to proceed with an information system's development. This needs to be contrasted with either the information systems people deciding what the eventual user needs and producing an information system for them, or the user demanding an information system without understanding what is possible or desirable from the different points of view of the other stakeholders.

Competitive advantage: This term is usually used to describe how one particular organisation attracts clients or customers when in competition with another. There are various sources of competitive advantage including low cost and differentiation.

Context marker: An aspect of the information systems development project which defines and delimits the business context. It is necessary for all the stakeholders to be involved in the identification of these.

Contingency: The contingency notion or concept states that it is not possible to be fully knowledgeable of the precise outcomes required from an information system at the outset of its development. As a result of this uncertainty information systems developers' plans can only be contingent on the current assumptions not changing. Once an assumption changes the development plan will need to reflect this change.

Continuous participative evaluation (CPE): Continuous participative evaluation implies:

1. A frequent evaluation of the information system's development

2. A participative evaluation process

3. A continuous focus on the business objectives of the information systems investment for the business

4. A continuous focus on the quality of the information system, including technological quality but not dominated by technology issues.

5. An acceptance that the objectives will evolve, influenced by management, external factors, organisational needs or information systems development problems.

Control techniques: A means of ensuring that the project is fully understood and that it remains on course.

Corporate memory: The ability of the organisation to recall useful information about techniques and procedures required to conduct its business. The term is sometimes associated with the notion of empowering staff to perform tasks requiring greater skills than they would otherwise be able to undertake.

Corporate strategy: A method through which the firm finds, gets and keeps its clients. In a broad sense it refers to how the firm relates to and interacts with its environment, including its stakeholders.

Cost avoidance: A technique used in cost benefit analysis which attempts to measure the various costs which an organisation will not have to incur when it acquires an information system.

Cost benefit analysis (CBA): The process of comparing the various costs associated with an investment with the benefits and the profits which it generates. Cost benefit analysis attempts to demonstrate whether the investment will earn a sufficient return in order for the organisation to consider it to be economically worth while. There are a number of different approaches to cost benefit analysis including cost displacement, cost avoidance, risk analysis etc.

Cost displacement: A technique used in cost benefit analysis which attempts to measure the various costs to which an organisation will no longer be committed when it acquires an information system. The new information system will be the cost and the benefits will be the expenses which the firm will no longer have to incur.

Critical success factors (CSF): Those aspects of the business which must be right for the enterprise to succeed in achieving its objectives. It is also sometimes said that even though all other aspects of the business are going well, if the critical success factors are not being achieved, then the business will not succeed.

Culture gap: Term to describe the high degree of misunderstanding and sometimes animosity between management and information systems groups.

Decision analysis: A technique used in cost benefit analysis which attempts to measure the impact of information systems on decisions made by individuals in the firm. Decision analysis is based on the proposition that better information can lead to better decisions which in turn can lead to better financial results.

Deliverables: The demonstrable results of a system or an initiative.

Direct cost: The cost incurred which may be shown as being incurred specifically due to some activity or project and not simply associated with the general overheads of the business. Direct costs vary in some proportion to the level of output.

Evaluation: In general terms evaluation can be described as the determination of the worth or value of something judged according to appropriate criteria.

Evaluation cycle: In the context of this book this refers to the different occasions during the software development cycle when evaluation takes place.

Evaluation gap: Failure for evaluation to be well performed when the initiators of the project become distanced from the development process and as a result the developers lose sight of the primary or business objectives of the information systems project. The gap is between the original criteria for success and the project management criteria eventually used.

Evaluation instrument: A formal document to collect evidence concerning the performance of an information system or the performance of the development of an information system.

Ex-ante: Refers to estimates of the benefits and the costs in advance of an investment.

Ex-post: Refers to the actual cost and estimates of the achieved benefits after the implementation of the investment.

Feedback loop: In the context of this book, the last part of the evaluation cycle in which documents are used as input to the next formative evaluation session to ensure that the business, financial and project pictures are not out of date or out of touch with the actual current requirements.

Formative evaluation: Formative evaluation is an iterative evaluation and decision making process continually influencing decisions about the information systems development process and the resulting information system. The term 'formative evaluation' has its origins in the evaluation of educational programmes and social programmes (Scriven 1967; Patton 1986). The phenomenon of formative evaluation is not new (Chelimsky 1985). It has been applied for many years in a number of disciplines with the roots of the concept stretching back into the nineteenth century. The word formative derives from to 'mould by discipline and education' (Shorter Oxford Dictionary, 1983). This is very close to the approach used by Walsham (1993) which he refers to as interpretative evaluation and which he highlights as an important facet in information systems management. This is also sometimes termed learning evaluation.

Framework: It is a fundamental structure for a system of ideas where a structure is a number of parts that are put together in a particular way.

Generic strategy: One of the basic ways in which a firm can find, get and keep its clients. According to Porter (1985) there are two generic strategies, which are *cost leadership* and *differentiation*. A generic strategy may be broad based or focused on a niche in the market.

Hard cost: Costs associated with an investment that are agreed by everyone to be directly attributable to the investment, and which can be easily captured by accounting procedures.

Hidden cost: A non-obvious cost associated with an investment that may in fact appear to be due to another source.

IBP (The initial business picture): The line managers and users' view or vision as to what the information system should achieve in order to help them attain their corporate goals.

IFP (The initial financial picture): The accountants and financial staff's view or vision as to what the information system should achieve in order to help them attain their corporate goals.

Intangible benefit: Benefits produced by an investment which are not immediately obvious and/or measurable in financial terms.

Internet: A global collection of interconnected computer networks consisting of mainframes, mid-range systems and personal computers.

IPP (The initial project picture): The information systems project staff's view or vision as to what the information system should achieve.

IT Benefit: The benefit produced by an investment in information technology. It is likely that such an investment will produce both tangible and intangible IT benefits.

IT Business benefits: This normally refers to advantages, profits or gains which are delivered by the use of information systems. This traditionally involves performing tasks faster, with fewer errors and producing higher quality output than could otherwise be achieved.

KPI (Key performance indicators): The metrics by which it is possible to ascertain if a CSF has been achieved. Thus if a CSF is the cost of production, the KPI would be the actual amount by which these costs have to be reduced.

Macro model: A high level model employing general concepts, or rough drawings, or imprecise fabrications to present a conceptual picture which will contextualise the problem or opportunity as well as provide a suggested solution.

Marginal cost: The cost associated with the production of one extra unit or the cost involved in a new activity excluding the general overhead.

Meso model: Adds some detail to a macro model, but will still be expressed primarily in generalities.

Meta-evaluation: The evaluation of evaluations.

Micro model: A detailed model which attempts to be closer to reality and thus to use more specific or life-like representations or values.

Model: A representation of an artefact, a construction, a system or an event or sequence of events.

Modernism: A belief that science provides a knowledge of reality which is exact and efficient and relevant to life in a modern society.

Moving goal-post syndrome (MGPS): The moving goal-post syndrome may be defined as the phenomenon which occurs when the organisation changes its goals or objectives within an assumed management time-frame. This phenomenon results in projects or programmes having to make rapid alterations to plans and actions to accommodate the changed circumstances, and is assumed by most managers to be undesirable and avoidable, if only the planning had been better. This assumption of stability in objectives is now increasingly seen to be unrealistic and *the phenomenon of the moving goal-post should now be seen as natural and necessary*, and appropriate management of moving goal-post methods should be adopted.

NPV (Net present value): is the difference between the sum of the values of the cash inflows, discounted at an appropriate cost of capital, and the present value of the original investment. Provided the NPV is greater than or equal to zero the investment will earn the firm's required rate of return.

Opportunity cost: The opportunity cost of an investment is the amount which the organisation could have earned if the sum invested in IT was used in another way.

Outcome: In the context of this book, the business result of the information system after it has been successfully commissioned and implemented.

Overhead cost: The overhead costs are the costs of running the business which do not vary directly with the level of output. Overhead costs tend to increase in step functions i.e. the increases are of relatively large amounts associated with such activities as acquiring an additional factory etc.

Outcome space: Using ABR, the information system is defined in broad business terms, largely in terms of benefits, which in some cases may be fairly general in nature. The term *outcome space* is used to describe these business benefits.

Participatory evaluation: An educational process through which the stakeholders produce action orientated knowledge about the nature and qualities of the information system and articulate their views and values to reach a consensus about future action.

Payback: The amount of time, usually expressed in years and months, required for an original investment to be repaid by the cash inflows.

Post-modernism: In the context of this book post-modernism is used to suggest new and somewhat experimental directions in management thinking, especially as it applies to information systems development.

Pre-modernism: A belief that the purpose of life is largely revealed through a divinity or that human understanding was a function of revealed truths. Life was also understood by direct reference to nature itself. In a pre-modern environment explanations of the world are either handed down by the church or they are subjective or personal and there is little accuracy or ability to predict or control.

Process: In the context of this book a process can be defined as a series of structured activities which are started at project initialisation and continue until project termination.

Risk: The possibility that the actual input variables and the outcomes may vary from those originally estimated.

Risk analysis: A technique used to assess the potential profitability of an investment. It involves the use of ranges as input variables rather than single point estimates. Probabilities may be associated with these ranges. The output of risk analysis is a profile of a series of possible results.

Ritual evaluation: Evaluation which is performed more for the form rather than actually being used to increase or improve the performance of a system.

ROI (Return on Investment): Accounting or financial management term to describe how well the firm has used its resources. It is usually calculated by dividing net profit after tax by total net assets.

Scope creep: The tendency for information systems projects to expand in order to embrace a wider range of issues than originally intended.

SDLC (Software development life cycle): The traditional approach to information systems development.

Soft cost: Costs associated with an investment that are not readily agreed by everyone to be directly attributable to the investment, and which are not easily captured by accounting procedures.

Stakeholder: Any individual with an involvement in the evaluation process. Can include senior management, users, financial managers, technical staff etc.

Strategic alignment: In the context of this book, strategic alignment refers to ensuring that the information systems effort of the organisation supports the overall corporate strategy.

Strategic evaluation: A necessary preparatory activity to strategic decision making at agreed milestones in the development cycle.

Strategic information system (SIS): An information system which helps a firm improve its long term performance by achieving its corporate strategy and thereby directly increasing its value added contribution to the industry value chain.

Strategic vision: How the top management of an enterprise believes it can achieve its objectives in the medium- to long-term.

Strategy: The formal use of this word refers to the way a firm finds, gets and keeps its clients. Common usage has reduced the meaning of strategy to be synonymous with plan. See also Corporate strategy and Generic strategy.

Summative evaluation: According to Finne *et al*, (1995) summative evaluation approaches typically aim at assessing outcomes and impacts; they take place towards the end of the programme or after its conclusion. They go on to point out that summative evaluations may be used conceptually, instrumentally, or persuasively. This means that the results of such an evaluation may be used to reconsider an investment proposal, to redirect investment efforts or to convince others that a new course of action is required.

Tactical evaluation: An iterative evaluation and decision making process integrated with the design of a system which incrementally directs the course of analysis and design for the information system.

Tangible benefit: Benefits produced by an investment which are immediately obvious and measurable. The term tangible benefit is usually used to refer to benefits which are directly reflected in the improvement in the profit performance of the organisation.

Target: That which the organisation intends to achieve. In the context of this book the targets are the expected benefits to be derived from the information system.

Vision: Sometimes referred to as Strategic Vision or Business Vision, this term refers to a view as to how the firm can successfully function in the marketplace in the medium- to long-term. It usually encompasses how the firm will find, get and keep its clients.

Index